CONQUERING INTIMIDATION

How To Overcome the Fear That Paralyzes Your Potential

Kate McVeigh

CONQUERING INTIMIDATION

⋙⋘

How To Overcome the Fear That Paralyzes Your Potential

Unless otherwise indicated, all Scripture quotations are taken from the *King James Version* of the Bible.

First Printing 2000
ISBN 0-89276-962-9

In the U.S. write:
Kenneth Hagin Ministries
P.O. Box 50126
Tulsa, OK 74150-0126
1-888-28-FAITH
www.rhema.org

In Canada write:
Kenneth Hagin Ministries
P.O. Box 335, Station D
Etobicoke (Toronto), Ontario
Canada, M9A 4X3

Chapter One

FEAR NOT

FEAR NOT

Fear thou not; for I am with thee: be not dismayed;
for I am thy God: I will strengthen thee; yea, I will
help thee; yea, I will uphold thee with the right hand
of my righteousness.

— Isaiah 41:10

The word *conquer* has several definitions — all of which are very interesting because they describe exactly what has to be done to drive intimidating fear out of our lives. Webster defines *conquer* as "to overcome by force, especially by force of arms; to gain control over by surmounting impediments; to overcome or surmount by mental or moral force; to be victorious: to win." I especially like those words, "to win," because we are going to win the war against intimidation and gain control over all of its negative aspects.

Sometimes it seems as though the devil focuses a great deal of his energy on trying to intimidate us, and many people, including Christians, struggle with fear and intimidation. Intimidation is not from God, and we must resist it in the power of the Holy Spirit. How? The only power that can meet and conquer intimidating fear is faith!

I am determined to be an overcomer in life, and I believe that's what you want too. When I decided to do a study on the subject of intimidation, I started by establishing the actual definition of the word *intimidate* in Webster's dictionary. I discovered that it means "to make afraid, to daunt, to force or detour with threats of violence." Think about that phrase — *to make afraid.*

Almost everyone has experienced some measure of intimidating fear in his or her life, and if you're anything like me, it wasn't a good feeling. In fact, I was surprised at just how many areas in my own life had been influenced in some respect by intimidation. It is tormenting and uncomfortable, and if we don't purpose in our hearts to conquer it, we will never accomplish much for God. Once I recognized the source of these negative feelings, I had to put a stop to it in my own life and try to help others whose potential greatness is yet to be tapped.

I don't want anything in my life to give the devil satisfaction, and I know he loves it when we're intimidated. In fact, I believe intimidation is one of his most powerful weapons. He delights when we shrink back from accepting God's great plan for our lives. He loves it when we timidly back away from doing anything that will significantly contribute to the advancement of God's kingdom on earth — whether it's pulpit ministry or joining the choir.

When we see ourselves as unqualified and insignificant, lacking confidence and feeling insecure, we play right into Satan's hands. Why do we let him influence us? What he tells us isn't important. It isn't even true! John 8:44 says there is no truth in him. He isn't capable of speaking the truth. So when he says, "You can't do that!" "Who do you think you are?" — he's lying! This Scripture goes on to say *...When he speaketh a lie, he speaketh of his own: for he is a liar, and the father of it.*

I remind myself often that Christ dwells in me — I am a new creature in Him who can do all things — and that includes conquering intimidation! But it doesn't just happen automatically, and one of the reasons is that it starts so early in our lives. By the time we're adults, if the Word of God hasn't renewed our minds, we're so used to feeling fearful and insecure that we don't know how to be any other way.

I'll use myself as an illustration of what I mean. I was placed in Special Education classes for slow learners as a fifth grader, and the result was a constant feeling of overwhelming intimidation — from teachers, peers, and practically everyone I met! I thought no one liked me because they perceived that I was dumb. Other kids made fun of me. And as if all of that were not enough, the braces on my teeth made me feel ugly!

The one thing that intimidated me most was the assignment I was given in school that involved being called upon to speak in front of people. I became so paralyzed with fear over having to give an oral book report, for example, that I nearly fainted! Then if I could actually recover enough to stand to my feet, my knees knocked together, my breathing accelerated, and by the time I opened my mouth, I sounded like Mickey Mouse with asthma. It was a nightmare, and I was miserable!

Growing up with athletic brothers, I learned to love basketball. We played basketball all the time at home, and I loved it! I could beat all the guys. At last I'd found some-thing I was good at. But at school, the girls on the basketball team so intimidated me by telling me I was stupid that my hands shook so badly that I made silly mistakes.

When I received the Lord at the age of sixteen as a result of my mother's amazing conversion and healing, my life was forever changed. I still had to work at overcoming intimidation — especially fear of man — but I learned about God's favor, and it began to work for me. I suddenly realized that God loved me, and I began to see myself as He sees me. I was no longer so timid, and my confidence was building.

Almost every time God challenges us to do something new — to take some new direction that is likely to stretch us beyond our natural capabilities — we may experience a measure of fear. Why? Because these changes have the potential to expose our weaknesses to others and to our-selves. But if God has called us to do something, we must believe that He will also provide whatever we need to see it through to a positive conclusion.

Proverbs 28:1 says...*the righteous are bold as a lion*. And intimidation can be conquered with boldness! *Yet amid all these things we are more than conquerors and gain a surpassing victory through Him Who loved us* (Romans 8:37). We have to stop allowing ourselves to be intimidated by the devil. It is a choice that we have to make. It often takes every ounce of courage and strength we can muster, but we must be willing to step out even if we're afraid!

When I felt strongly that God was leading me to leave my home and family in Michigan and go to Bible School in Oklahoma, I quickly developed a bad case of the "what ifs," — a classic fruit of the spirit of fear and intimidation. I loved my home church, and immediately — like a recording constantly playing in my mind — I started thinking, "What if I don't like it?" "What if I don't do well?" "What if I run out of money to pay for school?" "What if I don't meet anybody there?" "What if I don't make any new friends?"

No Place to Go but Up!

Sometimes those people you feel close to aren't all that helpful when the direction of your life seems to take an abrupt turn. When I quit my job in preparation for moving to Oklahoma to attend school, I tried to be confident. I told people, "I have no place to go but up!" But friends asked me how I was going to pay my bills. They asked what I would do way out there if school was too hard? What would I do after graduation if nobody ever invited me to preach?

Though I wasn't aware that I was taking steps to overcome my intimidation, I decided to compile a list of my own — some "what ifs" that were positive instead of negative. I asked myself, "What if I do great in school and get lots of invitations to speak?" "What if God meets all of my needs — spiritual, financial, social, and emotional?" "What if I succeed at everything I set my hand to?"

I've learned that most accomplishments in life come in steps or phases. You may not be where you want to be yet, but you also aren't where you used to be. That's one of the reasons it's important to avoid comparing ourselves with one another. We're always going to find somebody that looks like they're way ahead of us in the natural. Then there will be someone else who thinks we're way out there ahead of them.

Nothing is accomplished when we uselessly compare ourselves with one another. We need to believe and say, "God, I'm going to do what You've called me to do at the pace You've called me to do it, and I'm not going to compare myself with anyone else."

It takes the pressure off when we realize that God doesn't expect us to be like everyone else. He created us to be individuals. If everyone were exactly the same, we certainly wouldn't win many people to Christ. It takes all kinds of people to minister to the wide variety of individuals God places in our paths. Comparing yourself with others brings needless misery. Be yourself!

If you have ever felt intimidated in the presence of people you consider to be important, you will easily relate to this story.

Fear of Man

After I went to Bible School, I did receive invitations to minister. You may remember that speaking in front of people was a strong area of intimidation for me as a schoolgirl. Well, I started to preach, and I shook, quivered, and trembled, but remained determined to overcome the intimidation of people and hold on tightly to God's hand. I confessed Isaiah 41:13 over and over, ...*I the Lord thy God will hold thy right hand, saying unto thee, Fear not; I will help thee.*

I was especially intimidated in certain meetings where other ministers were gathered. I remember praying, "Lord, deliver me from being intimidated around my peers, and help me to overcome fear and to be bold!" And then I confessed, "I am the righteousness of God in Christ Jesus, and I am as bold as a lion!" Then I learned a very important lesson: we should be careful what we pray for.

Suddenly, well-known preachers and teachers were in almost every meeting I attended. When I prayed for God to deliver me, He sent me right into that situation! If I allowed the devil to get the best of me by taking over my thoughts, I would just fold up — and I couldn't do that!

Rev. Kenneth Hagin hosted a series of Holy Ghost meetings about that time, and I attended as many of those meetings as I could. One particular evening, after a day off that had turned into an entire day of shopping, I decided to slip into the meeting to hear some good preaching. I hadn't spent a lot of time in prayer that day. I hadn't even washed my hair! I thought, "This is my day off. I'm not going to have to do anything there. I'm just going to go over there and receive the Word of the Lord."

I grabbed a Bible on my way out the door and found a seat in the auditorium just as Brother Hagin stepped to the podium. He said, "The Lord is using women in ministry today..." I praised the Lord and thought, *I'm glad he said that. That's good news for me!*

Brother Hagin continued, "As a matter of fact, we're going to have a woman preach tonight." I thought, "Wow! Cool! I wonder who it is. This is going to be good."

He said, "Kate…" And my heart went *whomp*.

Then I thought, "Maybe there's another Kate out here somewhere. I sure hope so." But Brother Hagin said, "Kate McVeigh, come on up here and preach." Talk about intimidation trying to get a stronghold!

Once I recovered from the shock and finally stood to my feet, I started walking toward the front of the auditorium when someone reminded me that I didn't have my Bible, so I went back to my seat, grabbed my Bible, and took off. You can imagine what went through my mind when I got to the podium and realized that the Bible I had picked up as I ran out of the house was one of those daily devotional Bibles laid out with selected passages of Scripture from the Old and New Testaments, Psalms, and Proverbs. It isn't really designed as a reference book. It's a method of reading through the Bible in a year.

I knew I couldn't preach from that Bible! I wouldn't be able to locate scriptures quickly enough, so I didn't read them — I quoted them. Praise the Lord! He moved powerfully that evening, and after the first few minutes of crippling fear, I became very bold. I learned that God can do any-thing…through anyone…in spite of all kinds of uncomfort-able circumstances.

Just Do It!

One way to gain freedom from intimidation is to just do it…no matter how you feel. Whatever is intimidating us to the point of immobility, we must face it and decide to do it anyway.

I began to confess 2 Timothy 1:7,8 from The Amplified Bible all the time. *For God did not give us a spirit of timidity (of cowardice, of craven and cringing and fawning fear), but [He has given us a spirit] of power and of love and of calm and well-balanced mind and discipline and self-control. Do not blush or be ashamed then, to testify to and for our Lord…but do it in the power of God!* I love these Scriptures! I realized the cringing timidity I was experiencing while speaking in front of people didn't come from God, so I shouldn't be blushing with fear! I needed to get up and be bold about what God had called me to do.

The Fear of Man Will Bring a Snare

According to Proverbs 29:25 AMP, *The fear of man brings a snare, but whoever leans on, trusts in, and puts his*

confidence in the Lord is safe and set on high. When we allow ourselves to be intimidated by other people, we are only going to be able to go so far before we'll be jerked back by that snare. If you study the word *snare*, it refers to putting a snare, chain, or leash on a dog. That dog can only venture so far before it is jerked back by the tether around its neck. The progress of mobility is completely hindered.

It's the same with us. We can't worry about what other people are going to think about us. We must strive to do our best to please and be a blessing to people, but we cannot allow ourselves to become people-pleasers rather than God-pleasers. That is a dangerous trap. We must always give God first place. We can do things for people to help them out or just to make them happy, but if we do those things to keep them from becoming angry with us or to maintain their friendship, our motivation is entirely wrong. A relationship based on taking advantage of another person's willingness to be used is not a relationship worth maintaining.

Fear of man, fear of what people think about us, and fear of not being accepted hinder God's plan for our lives. The devil knows that and works hard to keep us in bondage to that fear.

One way to eliminate intimidation from your life is to see it for what it is — a manipulative lie of the enemy — confront it, and by faith, allow the Holy Spirit to walk you through it. You will experience victory as you commit to spending time in the Word, searching out scriptures that edify and encourage you, and speaking boldly what God's Word says about you. Start seeing yourself changed!

If you see yourself as a grasshopper, you'll remain a grasshopper. But if God sees a giant when He looks at you, you need to see yourself as a giant — well able to overcome the Goliaths of fear, intimidation, rejection, and insecurity that come against you. Your day of freedom from man-pleasing has come!

Ask yourself as the apostle Paul did in Galatians 1:10, *...do I now persuade men, or God? or do I seek to please men? for if I yet pleased men, I should not be the servant of Christ.*

David and the Intimidator

I'm sure you remember the story in 1 Samuel 17 of David and Goliath. Verses 4-7 describe exactly how intimidating Goliath was:

> *And there went out a champion out of the camp of the Philistines, named Goliath, of Gath, whose*

height was six cubits and a span. And he had an hel-
met of brass upon his head, and he was armed with
a coat of mail; and the weight of the coat was five
thousand shekels of brass. And he had greaves of
brass upon his legs, and a target of brass between his
shoulders. And the staff of his spear was like a
weaver's beam; and his spear's head weighed six
hundred shekels of iron: and one bearing a shield
went before him.

He was just a ten-foot-tall bully! He had already man-
aged to intimidate the entire army of Israel — including
King Saul — when he met the shepherd boy. David refused
to be intimidated even when Goliath promised to feed his
flesh to the birds and wild animals. Why? How had this
child developed such confidence in himself? In truth he
hadn't — David had developed confidence in his Lord.

David had been tending to his father's sheep. For long
periods of time he had no one but God to talk with. He
spent hour after hour with the Lord being built up in his
inner man. Sometimes he prayed and praised from morning
until night.

Over time, his relationship with the Lord enabled
David to confidently face a roaring lion and a scavenging

bear as they attempted to carry off sheep from his flock. With God's help, David had killed both. Facing the giant Goliath, David said, *Thy servant slew both the lion and the bear: and this uncircumcised Philistine shall be as one of them, seeing he hath defied the armies of the living God. David said moreover, The Lord that delivered me out of the paw of the lion, and out of the paw of the bear, he will deliver me out of the hand of this Philistine...* (vv. 36,37).

When our trust is placed in God, and we don't waver, He will help us just as he helped David conquer the lion, the bear, and Goliath. We can conquer fear and intimidation in the same way!

Who or what are the lions, bears, and giants that are hindering God's plan for your life? For me, intimidation usually visited me in the form of a person, so you can understand what a shock it was when God called me to preach. But 1 Corinthians 1:27 says that He's...*chosen the foolish things of this world to confound the wise....*

I really battled intimidation for years. I was afraid to preach, but I did it anyway. Sometimes the only way to break free from intimidation is to just do it — to purpose in your heart that whether or not your knees are knocking, you're going to do it anyway because you believe that you are free!

Now I speak in front of people nearly every week of my life, and it doesn't bother me at all. But I don't believe that I would experience the victory I have today had I not stepped out in faith yesterday.

One way to eliminate
intimidation from your
life is to see it for what
it is — a manipulative lie
of the enemy — confront it,
and by faith, allow the
Holy Spirit to walk
you through it.

Chapter Two

LETTING GO OF THE PAST

LETTING GO OF THE PAST

Remember ye not the former things, neither consider

the things of old. Behold, I will do a new thing; now

it shall spring forth; shall ye not know it? I will even

make a way in the wilderness, and rivers in the desert.

— Isaiah 43:18,19

Sometimes God wants to do a new thing in our lives

and make a way where there seems to be no way. Perhaps

you have cried, "Lord, I need change. I want change." But

you found that intimidation and fear are usually associated

with change so you decided not to go there. The truth is that

we might not know all the details of the future, but this

much we can be sure of: We know Who holds our future, and it's a good one (see Jeremiah 29:11). Intimidation must be conquered so we can step out in faith. Fear only holds us hostage! We need to remember that Jesus paid the ransom for all hostages to be released! Hallelujah!

Isaiah 41:10,13 says, *Fear thou not; for I am with thee: be not dismayed; for I am thy God: I will strengthen thee; yea, I will help thee; yea, I will uphold thee with the right hand of my righteousness. For I the Lord thy God will hold thy right hand, saying unto thee, Fear not; I will help thee.* God will hold our hands just as we would comfort a tearful child by taking his or her hand in ours. When a child is frightened, we say, "Don't be afraid. I'll hold your hand." That's the way God speaks to us when He's leading us in a new direction.

Change can be good. It can bring growth, joy, and newfound prosperity. We need to pray and discover the source of our fear of change.

For example, maybe the Lord is leading you to a new job or business venture, but you haven't acted on it because you've been at the same job for a long time, know the people, and have emotional ties to the familiarity of your tasks and surroundings.

Psalm 34:4 says, *I sought the Lord, and he heard me, and delivered me from all my fears.* Notice the psalmist said he was delivered from *all* of his fears. God does not want you to be afraid in *any* area of your life. He doesn't want you to be afraid of people, change, or anything else. He said, "All..." Webster's dictionary says the word *all* means "the total entity or extent of; the whole number, amount, or quantity of; the utmost possible; each and every thing." So *all* really means ALL!

It has been said that the Bible contains three-hundred-sixty-five "fear nots" — one for each day of the year! Every day of the year, you can get up and read a different "fear not" right out of the Word of God.

The Trust Factor

Again, God wants us to step out in faith and that requires trust that He will walk with us through the changes in our lives. I love Proverbs 3:5,6 in The Amplified Bible:

Lean on, trust in, and be confident in the Lord with all your heart and mind and do not rely on your own insight or understanding. In all your ways, know, recognize, and acknowledge Him, and He will direct and make straight and plain your paths.

If we're not careful, our own negative thoughts and negative input from others can cause us to become so fearful that we begin to doubt God. We can't allow ourselves to do that because it will paralyze His plan for our lives! We have to be filled with faith and trust in Him.

Some close friends of mine recently stepped out in faith and bought some property on which to construct a building to better accommodate their expanding carpet business. We prayed for the right property to be available for sale and claimed all that God wanted them to have. Even so, they experienced some challenging moments with the "what if" syndrome. *What if the money didn't come in for construction? What if changing locations caused customers to be unable to find them?*

Okay, but what if business was better than ever? What if trusting God and stepping out in faith brought in so many customers they could barely handle all of the new business? We'll never know some things until we factor in trust and step out in faith.

Aim High: Set Some Goals for Yourself

Do you not know that in a race all the runners compete, but [only] one receives the prize? So run [your race] that you may lay hold [of the prize] and make it yours.

— 1 Corinthians 9:24 AMP

The apostle Paul compared the Christian walk with athletic contests. I don't know about you, but I've never heard of a successful athlete who did not set goals and work hard toward achieving them. As Christians, we must do likewise.

You might ask, "But what if I set a whole lot of goals and don't reach *any* of them?" What if you set a whole lot of goals and reach *some* of them? It's better than setting no goals at all. I'd rather set lots of goals and reach half of them than to set no goals and reach all of them. It's always better to believe God and step out in faith. God will be right there with you — leading and guiding every step of the way. Don't be afraid to step out. God cares about everything that concerns you.

"I'm not Qualified"

Sometimes we feel as though God has called us to do something that we aren't qualified for. Have you ever felt that He was leading you into an area in which you didn't have enough experience? I know of several instances where

people have dealt with these issues, but God had called and anointed them to do a certain job, and they did it.

Did you know that you can do anything God has called you to do? Do you realize that you are neither too young nor too old or over- or under-qualified to be used by God? You're not even too "in-between" for God to use in ministry. When God called Jeremiah, he said:

> ...Lord God! behold, I cannot speak: for I am a child. But the Lord said...Say not, I am a child: for thou shalt go to all that I shall send thee and whatsoever I command thee thou shalt speak. Be not afraid of their faces: for I am with thee to deliver thee, saith the Lord.
>
> — Jeremiah 1:6-8

I certainly know what that scripture is talking about! I was a sixteen-year-old high school girl when God called me to preach the Gospel throughout America and in other nations. I sensed His call to preach from the very beginning of my new life in Christ. This was pretty serious for someone who nearly passed out over giving an oral book report!

Right away I contacted a young man whose opinion I respected for advice as to how I should respond to what I was sensing in my spirit. His immediate reaction was "God could never use you to preach!" Now, that might have threatened to bring back all of my old feelings of intimidation and insecurity, but instead, I thought, *No, I am sure about what God is saying to me, and I'm not going to get discouraged! I can do all things through Christ who strengthens me!*

I started studying and applying the simple principles of faith and confession that I had heard Brother Hagin teach at the crusade when I got saved. I spent hours every day listening to his tapes and walking my bedroom floor confessing, "I have the mind of Christ. The Greater One lives in me. Greater is He that's in me than he that is in the world!" (See 1 John 4:4)

The first book I ever read from beginning to end was *The Believer's Authority* by Brother Hagin. And when I did, I suddenly realized that I had a new ability to comprehend what I read. So I got all of Brother Hagin's books I could find and studied them with a vengeance.

I committed scriptures to memory and made positive confessions over my life every day. I even looked at an empty calendar and confessed, "One day you won't be large enough to write in all the places that God will send me!" I may not have been qualified in the traditional sense of the word, but God had qualified me and was preparing me for my purpose.

Everything Isn't Always As It Appears

I recently spoke with someone I had met when I was a teenager. He didn't appear to be any smarter than anyone else when we were growing up. We talked and prayed together about all kinds of things in those days, and he seemed to be just an average guy. But now he's a millionaire who owns his own company! When the anointing of God comes on your life, it doesn't matter if you *feel* qualified or not. If God is calling you to do something, then you can step out in faith and do it. Things are not always as they *appear* to be.

When my radio ministry started a few years ago, I remember thinking, *I can't go on radio! I don't know how to do that! What if the money doesn't come in?* It seemed as though the Holy Spirit was saying, "You'll never know until you try. What if it does come in?" So I decided to trust God. I may have known nothing about radio, and I may have appeared to be unqualified to have a radio program — but God anointed my radio ministry, and now we're on radio stations around the country, and we're preparing to start a television program.

Some people say, "I don't feel particularly called to serve in a certain area." If you give it to God and He anoints you, you cannot fail. You may not be the brainiest person in the pew, but if you have the anointing of God, failure is not an option. I'd rather listen to an anointed singer than someone with a highly trained voice but no anointing. How about you?

Confidence to Step into the Unknown

I know some people whose confidence comes from alcohol and drugs. Those things are only temporary fixes for a deeper problem. Our confidence must come from knowing that God has a good plan for our lives and that He will bring it to pass.

Because I became determined to preach at times when I was literally so frightened I could barely speak, I can do it now without being nervous at all. My confidence grew as a result of trusting God, giving myself time, gaining experience, and conquering fear of people.

I like what 2 Timothy 1:7 says, *For God hath not given us the spirit of fear; but of power, and of love, and of a sound mind.* I especially like to study that scripture from The Living Bible: *For the Holy Spirit, God's gift, does not want you to be afraid of people, but to be wise and strong, and to love them and enjoy being with them.*

Whenever fear was about to paralyze me, I quoted that scripture regularly, along with John 14:27 in The Amplified Bible, *...[Stop allowing yourselves to be agitated and disturbed; and do not permit yourselves to be fearful and intimidated and cowardly and unsettled].*

Faith Comes by Hearing — Does Fear?

Romans 10:17 says that faith comes by hearing, so how hard is it to figure out that fear can also come by hearing? As long as we keep hearing bad reports and listening to all the terrible things that happen to people, sooner or later we can be affected. For example, not long ago I started hearing a lot about a flu virus that seemed to be attacking lots and lots of people. The way folks talked, you would have thought there wasn't a person in the country who didn't have the flu!

Everywhere I went people wanted to know if I was going to get a flu shot. Now, I'm not telling anyone not to get flu shots. But I said, "Yes, I'm taking my flu shot from Psalm 91:10, *...neither shall any plague come nigh my dwelling.*

I'm not going to get the flu. Instead, I am declaring that no plague shall come near my dwelling."

During this time, I noticed that people were intimidated by even a threat of flu. They talked about it so much that it sounded as though they were hoping for the worst. *You know the flu is going around. I'll probably get it like everybody else.*

Why don't we try saying, "I'm not going to get the flu! If anybody's not going to get the flu this year, it's going to be me." The "F" in fear stands for false. The "E" stands for evidence. The "A" stands for appearing. And the "R" stands for real. What then is fear? It is False Evidence Appearing Real. It's a lie dressed up as the truth!

When fear comes knocking at your door, you need to let faith answer. I like what one person said, "Fear knocked, faith answered, and nobody was home." God wants us to be delivered from fear in every single area of our lives. We must learn to resist fear!

Resist the Devil at His Onset

Have you ever felt symptoms of a cold coming on? It doesn't seem like anything terribly serious, and you don't even think to pray about it. Then someone asks you how you feel, and you respond, "I'm fine. I just have the sniffles." Three days later, you feel awful, grab your Bible, and start speaking to that cold, commanding healing to come.

The minute you noticed the sniffles, you should have started to resist them with the Word of faith. We must learn to resist sickness and discouragement at its onset. We can't wait until we're down and out. Second Corinthians 10:5 instructs us to cast down imaginations, take every thought captive, and bring it into the obedience of Christ. But many times we let our imaginations (thoughts) cast us down, and we become the captives!

People are always discussing statistics. They talk about this or that happening to seventy-five percent of the population every year. Or fifty percent of everybody in the country experiences this or that at least once in their lifetime. What would happen if you decided to be part of the twenty-five percent that it doesn't happen to? What if you said, "I'm going to be on the fifty percent side of the country that won't experience this."

Why do we always think we're going to be on the wrong end of the stick? We should be claiming to be the one that the statistic never touches.

Several years ago the TV news carried a story of a tiger that was loose in the Detroit suburb where my family lives. Things around there got a little crazy because suddenly everybody thought the tiger would be in *their* backyard. Fear came by hearing...the news!

I really believe that we allow fear of failure, rejection, people, or whatever to seize our hearts before we take the time to recognize the devil as its source. James 4:7 tells us, *Submit yourselves therefore to God. Resist the devil, and he will flee from you.* One definition of the word *flee* says, "to run as in terror." I like to think of the devil fleeing in terror from me!

Another translation says we are to resist him at his onset (see 2 Peter 5:9 AMP) — the moment fear or intimidation or anything along those lines tries to attach itself to our mind.

When people travel to other countries, they are required to go through customs. A series of questions are asked and security people scan all the luggage, making sure that nobody brings anything into that country that doesn't belong there. What if we set up our own spiritual "customs agency" when thoughts come against our mind? We could scan those thoughts and say, "Wait a minute, is this good? Is this pure? Is this lovely? Is this a good report?" Why?

Philippians 4:8 says ...*if there be any virtue, and if there be any praise, think on these things.* If it's not a good report, don't let it through to your heart. Don't let it come to stay in your country, so to speak.

Fear begins with a thought in your mind. Then the devil comes along and asks, "What are you going to do? What are you going to do? What are you going to do?" Has anyone ever asked you that when you were faced with a problem? Say you lost your job for some reason. *What are you going to do?* The truth is you don't have to know what you're going to do, but you can trust God. You can stand on His Word. You can believe that God will make a way.

Perhaps you or someone you love has been given a terrifying health report from the doctor. Immediately people want to know what you're going to do. You can say, "I'm going to believe God's Word." We need to take hold of those thoughts the minute they come.

Faith comes by hearing and hearing and hearing. We need to listen and listen and listen. Don't listen to fear. Be bold and strong. When you conquer intimidation, you can do anything God calls you to do.

What if we set up our own spiritual "customs agency" when thoughts come against our mind? We could scan those thoughts and say, "Wait a minute, is this good? Is this pure? Is this lovely? Is this a good report?"

Chapter Three

DEFEATING INSECURITY

DEFEATING INSECURITY

Stand fast therefore in the liberty wherewith Christ hath made us free, and be not entangled again with the yoke of bondage.

— Galatians 5:1

Have you ever experienced a lack of self-confidence, uncertainty, or instability? Have you ever been so upset that you thought you might drown in a pool of anxiety? This is how the word *insecurity* is defined. It leaves us feeling unsafe, threatened, and apprehensive. But God's Word and His will for you and me is to walk in victory over insecurity. God wants us to be secure and confident in Him, having no fear of failure.

We know that the chief author of insecurity is the devil, but the Word lets us know that we can walk in victory over insecurity by God's grace and become all that He has called us to be. I looked up the word *secure* to determine exactly what it meant before getting into this chapter.

Of course, *secure* is just the opposite of *insecure*. *Secure* is described as "free from danger, harm, or risk of loss. Free from fear, anxiety, or doubt; confident; not likely to fail or give way; stable, assured, certain; guarded from danger, harm or risk of loss; so strong or well made as to render loss, escape or failure impossible." That sounds like holy boldness to me!

The world teaches us to have confidence, and we need to be confident. But our confidence should be in who God made us to be. Real confidence and trust has to be in God and not in ourselves because we can't always help ourselves.

We are often told that we can trust only ourselves, but have you ever failed yourself? Are you able to heal your sick body? Can you deliver yourself from fear? Only God can do these things, so our trust must be in Him.

Christ is My Security

Two months after I got saved, the new school year began. As you know, school had always been painful for me, and on the outside, things seemed to be the same that first day of school. I returned to special education classes and started practicing with the same basketball team. But everything had changed inside me, and it took no time for everyone to start noticing it.

My teachers were astounded by the change in my academic performance. Concepts that previously confused and frustrated me were suddenly simple to grasp. When I was asked what had happened to me, I quickly responded, "I have the mind of Christ now. I've been born again!"

My turnaround on the basketball court was also astonishing to both coach and teammates. My newfound confidence in Jesus caused me to be able to concentrate on playing the sport. I had natural athletic ability that immediately became evident. By the end of the season, I was not only off the bench and in the game, but voted "Most Valuable Player"!

My old insecurities had been nailed to the cross of Christ, my Savior! I was no longer intimidated by what other people thought about how I used to be. Nothing mattered more than pleasing Jesus. Other kids actually wanted to be around me, and wanted me to become their "teacher" — leading them to the One who had set me free!

Some psychiatrists maintain that people who are born-again just use religion or God as a crutch because they don't have any confidence. I don't know about you, but I admit that I'm guilty of using God as a crutch. I lean on Him all the time, and I believe all of us need to lean on Him — especially in the hour in which we live.

My academic progress was a direct result of leaning and depending on the Lord. It was so remarkable that by the end of my junior year, I had been completely reintegrated into normal classes. And I continued to experience the Holy Spirit's supernatural increase my senior year. My last year of high school was marked by excellent grades.

Plant Seeds of Faith for a Harvest

Allow me to encourage you to start planting seeds of faith now — with your words and prayers — for the future. For example, I recently received a letter from a ministry with which I am familiar regarding their plan to purchase an office building. I knew in my heart that somewhere down the road — perhaps five or ten years from now — I would need my own office building for some of the things God has laid on my heart to do.

So I decided to plant my faith now for the future, and I sowed a seed toward their office building. I said, "Lord, I'm sowing this seed so that when I have need of more office space, the money is going to be there and that need is going to be met."

When I was just a young girl, the Lord laid on my heart that I was to go and visit elderly residents of nursing homes. The Lord said specifically, "If you do this now, you'll never be lonely when you're old." At the ripe old age of sixteen, I spent time visiting people in nursing homes every week. I said, "Lord, I'm sowing seed for my future, and I know that if Jesus should tarry and I live to be ninety years old or more, I'll never be lonely."

Be Anxious for Nothing

As the year two thousand began, statistics revealed that the United States was home to more than one hundred thousand citizens over the age of one hundred. Interestingly, a study of their longevity revealed that they hadn't necessarily eaten healthy, taken vitamins, exercised on a regular

basis, lived in a moderate climate, or any of the other sug-gestions we've been given to stay healthy and live long lives.

Some of them hadn't really taken very good care of their bodies at all. One thing they had in common, though, was that they hadn't allowed anxiety, worry, and intimidat-ing fear to consume them! Isn't that interesting?

Insecure people worry all the time. But that's not what the Word says to do. It says:

Be careful for nothing; but in every thing by prayer and supplication with thanksgiving let your requests be made known unto God. And the peace of God, which passeth all understanding, shall keep your hearts and minds through Christ Jesus.

— Philippians 4:6,7

People worry about everything — many without real-izing that God's plan for us includes the ability to live peace-ful lives. My relationship with the Lord has brought me so much peace and enjoyment. I had to learn to let go of some things that tried to disrupt my peace, but once I realized that I had a choice to be either peaceful or nervous and upset, I chose peace. Who wouldn't rather have peace?

The devil knows that worry and anxiety are tormenting, so he tries to see to it that we don't run out of situations and circumstances that have potential to create chaos. It seems as though when people think they have run out of things to worry about, the first thing they do is worry about what someone thinks about them. *Is he mad at me? She doesn't like me. What do they think of me? I wasn't asked to the get-together. What am I going to do?*

Insecure people tend to read things into words, actions, or situations that aren't even there. What difference does it make what someone else thinks about you? If they really were thinking evil of you, they wouldn't want you to know it because they are aware that they shouldn't be thinking those things anyway.

The insecure person worries about little things that most people don't even think to worry about. And it seems that women are especially tempted in this area. *Will other people like my hair this way? What color should I dye it?*

I found two gray hairs and immediately started thinking about dyeing my hair! Thank God, I did not think about what anyone else would say about it, but insecure women would have worried about that. They need to get over it and realize that God made them the way they are. He gave them their personality.

Freedom from insecurity and intimidation involves a decision in your heart that fear, worry, and anxiety have no place in your life in any way, shape, or form. First Peter 5:7 reminds us that we can cast all of our care upon Him. Why? Because He cares for us. If you study that word *cast*, it literally means, "to throw off." I really like The Amplified Bible's translation of this scripture:

> *Casting the whole of your care [all your anxieties, all your worries, all your concerns, once and for all] on Him, for He cares for you affectionately and cares about you watchfully.*

The Cares of the World

In His parable of the sower described in Mark 4:19, Jesus spoke of the cares of this world hindering our ability to receive from God.

> *Then the cares and anxieties of the world and distractions of the age, and the pleasure and delight and false glamour and deceitfulness of riches, and the craving and passionate desire for other things creep*

in and choke and suffocate the Word, and it
becomes fruitless.

— Mark 4:19, AMP

If you're allowing worry, anxiety, and care to stay on you, I urge you to throw it off quickly. It may try to jump back on you five minutes later, but just throw it off again. And keep throwing it off!

When we go to great lengths to plant the Word of God in our hearts, we cannot allow worry, fear, and anxiety to uproot and overtake it. We have to purpose in our hearts that we're going to be carefree.

I was speaking with someone on the phone the other day, and they concluded our conversation by saying, "Take care," immediately followed by, "No, wait a minute! Don't take care. Jesus doesn't want you to take care. He wants you to be free from care and worry." Amen!

Do You Have a Cat on Your Head?

I once heard a minister tell a story about his pet cat. As this person or other family members walked through the house, all of a sudden this cat would come flying through the air out of nowhere and land on their head! He said it didn't take long before they would grab that cat and throw it off.

This is a great illustration of how we are to cast off our cares. Wouldn't we look silly walking around with a cat stuck to our head? There are lots of people carrying the "cat" of care on their face or in their countenance. Everyone can see it. Even the psalmist David dealt with it, *Why art thou cast down, O my soul? and why art thou disquieted within me? hope thou in God: for I shall yet praise him, who is the health of my countenance, and my God* (Psalm 42:11).

God says to throw it off — get rid of it! Don't allow worry in your life. The Bible stresses that we shouldn't be troubled nor have any anxiety about anything because care and worry can ruin our lives.

Distractions

Are you sensing God moving like never before? At the same time, have you felt as though the enemy were attacking you lately? Why do you think you're under attack? Because God has something great in store for you or the devil wouldn't be trying so hard to discourage you. I believe the devil's goal is to distract you from what God has called you to do!

Distraction simply means "something that draws your attention away; to harass." The devil will bring certain things into your life to draw your attention away from what

God wants you to do, and he'll bring that distraction as harassment against you.

The Wasp Story

Since we have been discussing distractions and to what great lengths the devil will go to see that they invade our peaceful lives, I'll confide a personal story that seems ridiculous even as I attempt to put it into words. I once was plagued by a terrible fear of wasps! In fact, I was watching one of my favorite teachers minister a great message on TV on the subject of fear when a wasp came flying right by my head…in my house!

I had been having some problems with wasps building nests around the house, and nobody had figured out why they were so attracted to me! I had gotten so upset about these wasps that I had told my mother I was going to move! That seems like a drastic measure to take to avoid insects, but there it is. I knew, of course, that nobody can really run from their problems, but at the same time, I was tired of these wasps invading my space, and I had decided it was them or me — one of us was moving!

I was so upset about the wasp flying around in my house that I called my mother, and she turned into one of those 911 emergency operators, encouraging me to kill the thing. I could never kill them. In the past, I'd always called someone at my office to come over and kill them for me. But Mother was trying to talk me through this and keep me calm.

Mother said, "Now, Kate, you can do this. You can do it afraid. That wasp is more afraid of you than you are of it. Go get your can of Raid, and I'm going to help you." You should have seen me. I ran around after that silly thing with my Raid can in one hand and the phone in the other. I finally conquered that little thing — as well as my fear of wasps — once and for all. I overcame my insecurity with regard to the insect kingdom, and though I still don't like them, I can take control of the situation before it gets completely out of hand.

The Golf Issue

There may be certain things you like that someone else doesn't. So what? You may like to do certain things that other people don't like to do. It's not really a problem. Not long ago I seemed to be surrounded with friends — both in the ministry and in secular positions — who liked golfing. So I decided that I was going to like to golf.

My father loves golf, so he was thrilled when I took an interest. I bought clubs and a bag to haul them around in and decided to be as excited as everyone else seemed to be about golf. On the golf course, I tried to act like I knew what I was doing, but soon it became very clear that I did not. When I picked a club and my dad said, "Don't use that one," I replied, "I'm just cleaning it off." I'd pick another one, and if he didn't correct me, I would proceed. *I was determined to like to golf.*

It was not long before I had to admit that I didn't like playing golf. I couldn't stand this sport. I hadn't wanted anyone to know I didn't like it because it seemed so important to them, and I didn't want to be thought of as strange. Now I feel confident enough to let people go on and on about the great game of golf, and when they're finished, I can tell them I don't care for it myself. But give me a basketball and I'm happy.

We need to be confident and purpose in our hearts that we're going to like what we like, let others like what they like, and not worry about what anyone thinks. Now, I love golf — when somebody who really likes it is playing.

The Clothes Issue

Have you ever been shopping with someone who just keeps telling you they don't like the clothes you're trying on? You pick something out, try it on, look in the mirror, and you really like the outfit. It looks good on you, and you feel good about yourself in it.

Your friend stands back and, since you like the outfit so much, you're sure she's going to tell you how great it looks on you — but she says something like, "I really don't think that's your color." Or, "That makes you look a little frumpy." *Frumpy!?!?!?!*

Not long ago, someone told me that a mutual acquaintance of ours had commented about not liking the way I dress. I thought, "Hum. What am I doing wrong? I buy nice dresses and suits. I like them. I pick them out myself." But the thought that someone didn't like my clothes kept knocking around in my head. *Maybe I should look for something else.*

All of a sudden, I said, "I don't care if she doesn't like the way I dress. I like the way I dress and that's what matters."

We need to be confident in what we like and what we do. Be encouraged to be yourself — the individual God made you to be. Don't try to be somebody else. Don't spend precious time and effort wishing you were someone else. There is something special about every person. There's something about you that is unlike anyone else — a uniqueness and a wonderful "something special."

Be Yourself

When I first started preaching, I thought, "I'm not like so-and-so over here. And I don't preach just like so-and-so over there either." And people would ask, "Well, who do you preach like?" I really didn't know. Then the Lord said, "I don't want you to be like him. And I don't want you to preach like her. I want you to preach like you, and I want you to be you. I want you to be Kate. Don't try to be somebody else. Be yourself — the best you that you can be — and be proud of who I made you to be."

Don't let the devil rob you with insecurity. Believe in your heart that God knows everything about you, and purpose this day that you are going to be secure in who you are and in what God has called you to do.

My relationship with the
Lord has brought me so much
peace and enjoyment.
I had to learn to let go of
some things that tried to
disrupt my peace, but once I
realized that I had a choice to
be either peaceful or nervous
and upset, I chose peace.

Chapter Four

DECIDE TO BE DECISIVE

DECIDE TO BE DECISIVE

Multitudes, multitudes in the valley of decision....

— Joel 3:14

Insecure people who haven't conquered intimidation are indecisive. They are simply unable to make decisions. I've been there. How about you? Have you ever found yourself unable to decide what you want to eat and where? You meditate and vacillate. It's ridiculous! I used to second guess my decisions and change my mind a lot. I know what you're thinking — *that's because you're a woman!* (Smile)! You're probably right. Anyway, we need to just decide to be decisive — make a decision and stick with it. Indecision is a waste of precious

time. We accomplish more with less effort when we become decisive.

We often waste so much time wondering if we've made the right decision. We need to believe for wisdom in making decisions, and then act like we have it. Sometimes, when I am not sure about a decision, I just decide not to decide right now — if it can wait. I have found that deciding not to decide right now is a decision.

It's Okay to Delegate

Our ministry hosts an annual luncheon in my hometown. Each year the number of reservations increases, and we need more help to handle all of the details. Volunteers perform a very important function by greeting and checking in the two or three hundred people who paid good money to come through the door. I can't do all of that myself and remain spiritually prepared for the meeting.

They do such a great job that I don't even think about it anymore. I know each person is going to feel welcome and appreciated as they walk in, and that frees me to do my part. I allow my mother to decide on the menu because she is better at those things than I am.

I can delegate these tasks because I know God has anointed each of us for the responsibility we've been given. It's an answer to prayer. We have to make a quality decision that we cannot do everything ourselves. But fear of failure traps thousands in a "never-never land" of indecision.

We can't be afraid to make mistakes, or we'll never do anything. Important lessons can be learned from past mistakes — I emphasize past mistakes — not past failures! Making a mistake doesn't mean you're a failure. You weren't the first person who ever made a mistake, and you sure won't be the last one.

Right now, you could be the answer to prayer for your pastor, but he can't read your mind. Insecure people say, "They need to ask me. I'd love to do that, but I'm just waiting to be asked." Don't be vague and indecisive. Just go and tell your pastor what's in your heart. Tell him or her that you feel God is prompting you to volunteer for some task at the church.

Your pastor will be grateful, and you will be blessed as you serve the Lord by serving other people. Make a decision to put your hands to something for God. I believe every single Christian ought to be doing something for God, whether it's ushering, greeting, cleaning, singing, operating the prayer line, making calls, or cooking meals for people. Whatever you're good at, do it for God. If you don't know what to do, just do something until you do know.

Do What You Know 'til you Know What to Do

Lately I've noticed that more people seem to have difficulty deciding where to attend church. I often tell them to at least go somewhere that preaches the Word until they know. Keep yourself built up in the Word and in a position to be fed until you feel God has given you direction. I meet people all the time who request my recommendations on where to go to hear the Word of the Lord. My recommendations aren't important. Allow God to lead you, but in the meantime, keep pursuing a church home. You will know in your "knower" when you have found it. Once you have found your church, be faithful to your pastor and church, and you will be blessed!

How to Hear from God

Insecure people doubt their ability to hear from God. Have you ever wondered, "God, is that really You? If I knew it was really, really, really, really, really, *really* You, God, I would move." Have you been there? I remember when God was prompting me to have our ministry give somebody a large offering. It just kept coming up in my spirit. You usually know it's God when it keeps coming back and doesn't go away.

This kept coming up in my spirit, and I'd say, "All right, Lord, if that's You, show me again." Out of nowhere the thought would come back to my remembrance, *sow that seed.* "God, now if that's really, really You, please show me," I'd say. I'd go to church and the pastor would say, "If God's moving on your heart to give to somebody, do it."

Obviously, God was trying to get through to me, but I kept saying, "Lord, I'd do it if I just knew that I knew this was You because I know that You would bless me." A secure person realizes that he or she can hear from God.

Now, let's say I finally gave the money (I did), and I was blessed as a result. If God is dealing with you about something similar to this scenario, think about this. Maybe God prompts you to give somebody ten dollars, and you don't know if this is God or you — think about the consequences if you did do it. What would be so bad about giving someone ten dollars even if it wasn't God? What would happen to you? You would get blessed!

Second Corinthians 9:7 in The Amplified Bible says, *Let each one [give] as he has made up his own mind and purposed in his heart, not reluctantly or sorrowfully or under compulsion, for God loves (He takes pleasure in, prizes above other things, and is unwilling to abandon or to do without) a cheerful (joyous "prompt to do it") giver [whose heart is in his giving].*

If you're really seeking God and you still go the wrong way, He is able to get you back on track. It's when we never acknowledge Him that we mess up. It's when we don't go before the Lord and seek Him.

Proverbs 3:6 says we are to acknowledge God in all of our ways, and He will direct our paths. We get into trouble when we stop acknowledging Him and try to do everything ourselves.

Some people never acknowledge God in critical areas of their lives. They don't ask God for wisdom, for direction, and to show them certain things. Why? They don't believe He will. And they don't believe they can hear God telling them what to do. So instead, they just throw up their hands and don't ask God anything because they aren't convinced that He will show them what to do. I learned from my pastor to pray for wisdom every day to make the right decisions. What a difference this makes.

Faith believes it receives *before* it sees. And if you're going to be a person of faith, you have to purpose in your heart to believe the Word of God. James 1:5 says, *If any of you lack wisdom, let him ask of God, that giveth to all men liberally, and upbraideth not; and it shall be given him.* He will, will, will... God will freely give us wisdom.

Verse 6 goes on to say, *But let him ask in faith, nothing wavering. For he that wavereth is like a wave of the sea driven with the wind and tossed.* If you ask God for wisdom, you need to ask Him in faith and stop saying you don't know what to do.

I read those verses in James to people in prayer lines who need God's wisdom to make a decision. I suggest that they stand on James 1:5 and 6, and then I pray for God to show them what to do. Time and time again, I've seen someone walk up to them five minutes later and ask, "Well, you've been prayed for now. Do you know what to do?" And the person I'd prayed over said, "I don't know." Your confession ought to be, "God is revealing it to me," "I believe I know," or "I hear the voice of the Good Shepherd."

People come up and ask for wisdom and leave church saying, "I still don't know what I'm going to do." You ought to believe you received that wisdom in the prayer line! You should believe you're going to know what to do in time to make the correct decision.

The Lord once said to me, "You asked Me for wisdom, but you're still going around saying you don't know what to do." He said, "Do you believe that you received when you asked me for wisdom?" I said, "Yes." He said, "Then stop saying you don't know what to do and start saying you know what to do, because I'm revealing it to you. The Bible says My sheep know My voice. You ought to go around saying, 'I know the voice of God. I hear the voice of God. I'm a child of God. They that are led by the Spirit of God are the sons of God. God's children know His voice.'"

You can be led by the Spirit of God. You can know which way to go in your life. God will speak to you and you will hear Him. The insecure person says, "God won't talk to me." Recognize that for exactly what it is — a lie from the pit of hell!

God cares as much about you as He does me, your pastor, or anybody else. He wants to speak to you and direct you in areas of your life just like He speaks to us and directs us. Start saying that you do know what to do, that you hear the voice of the Good Shepherd, and no other voice will you follow.

True Joy comes from God

I travel all over the world, and sometimes I run across people who look familiar that I've met at a church somewhere. But I don't always remember them. I attended a rather large meeting one time where I wasn't preaching, and at the end of the service a lady came up and said, "Hello, I know you saw me, but you didn't want to talk to me. You walked right past me and ignored me."

I told the lady how very sorry I was and said, "I didn't see you." She said, "I know you did, but that's okay. I forgive you." I might have *looked* at her, but I didn't see her. In fact, I really didn't know her. She was just one out of a thousand in a church where I had preached. It wasn't possible that I would remember her. The insecure person immediately thinks you don't like her or him. Even after I told her that I had not seen her, she thought I was lying. Be careful not to read things into what other people say or do. You need to be bigger than that. Don't let your joy come from other people and how they treat you.

Your joy needs to come from the Lord within you. To be a secure person, your trust has to come from God. Another person can't fill that void in your heart. The attention of people isn't going to make you happy. Only God can make you happy and full of joy.

We Need to Like Ourselves

Matthew 19:19 tells us to love our neighbor as ourselves. We need to like ourselves. It is a big key to overcoming insecurity. A lot of people say very negative things about themselves. "I'm just no good." "I'm never going to amount to anything." "I'm just ugly." "I can't do that." "Nothing good ever happens to me!"

Why do we say negative things about ourselves that would hurt us if spoken by another person? When other people say terrible things about us, we get angry, but we let awful words come out of our own mouth about ourselves!

We must learn to speak better of ourselves. We need to learn to love and forgive ourselves. We cannot effectively love our neighbor if we do not love ourselves. When we are strong and confident in the Lord, we are encouraging to others and to ourselves because we know who we are in Christ.

We can't reach out to somebody in trouble and lift him or her up when we're beaten down with depression or a negative opinion of ourselves. It's hard to lift up another who is weak when we are also weak.

That's why God wants you to be confident and secure. He wants you to learn to like yourself…even to love yourself.

I changed some confessions in my life. One thing I always confessed was that I couldn't lose weight. One day the Lord said, "Quit saying you can't lose weight. You can do all things through Christ who strengthens you." Now I confess that I can be all that God's called me to be.

By faith I started looking in the mirror and calling those things that were not as though they were. I've never been seriously overweight, but like most women, I always feel that losing a few pounds would be a great boost. So I started to take a closer look at what I was eating and began saying, "I weigh such and such. I have no problem losing weight when I need to." This went on for a while, and after a relatively short period of time, when I stepped on the scale, I had lost several pounds. I thought, "Wow! This stuff works!"

Faith without works is dead according to James 2:17. The Amplified Bible says, *So also faith, if it does not have works (deeds and actions of obedience to back it up), by itself is destitute of power (inoperative, dead).* Start calling those things that are not as though they were in your life. Start saying that you're a secure person. Start saying that you're confident. Start saying that the Greater One lives in you. And start saying that you can and do make wise decisions!

Decide to Walk in Love

One of the best decisions we can make is to forgive those who have hurt us and to pray for them. Matthew 5:44 says to ...*pray for them which despitefully use you, and persecute you.*

I learned this early in my Christian walk. I was so "on fire" for the Lord after I got saved that I witnessed to everyone in my high school who would listen. Lots of people did listen, but one girl in my school who had caused me great pain and hurt in the past remained a "thorn in my flesh." Frankly, I didn't care if she ever got saved! Obviously, I really needed to make a decision to forgive this girl.

My mother knew about the bitterness in my heart toward this girl. So she told me about a book she had read that greatly changed a similar situation she had once gone through.

This book talked about forgiveness and praying for one's enemies. My mom related to me a very important key: If a person prays for his enemies, his feelings will eventually line up with the love of God in his heart.

So I decided to follow this advice and pray for the girl every day. It wasn't long before I began to feel a real love for her. I knew in my heart that I had truly forgiven her.

Then one day not long after I had started praying, she showed up at my house. It was definitely a surprise to see her standing on my front porch! She said, "I just happened to be in your neighborhood and wanted to ask you a question. Kate, what has happened to you? You've really changed."

"I asked Jesus to be my Savior," I replied. "Jesus opened my eyes and filled me with His love."

I shared with her how she could experience the same life-changing peace through a personal relationship with Jesus. That afternoon I was able to pray with that girl who had hurt me so much in the past. She was gloriously saved and filled with the Holy Ghost right there in my house!

The girl also told me that she had a problem with her knee that was going to require surgery. So I laid hands on her to pray, and the power of God hit her so hard that she fell to the floor. When she got up, she was totally healed!

Your decision to pray for someone who has hurt you opens the door for the Lord to do something great through you.

Another incident that involved my little hurt feelings came along after I had been in ministry for several years. I was really upset about something someone had said about me. I was talking with my mother on the telephone while I fixed my hair. I have a lot of hair, and I had a lot more then than I have now. I was "picking" it and telling my mom how this person had really done me wrong. I was having what one preacher calls "a fit of carnality." Have you ever had one of those?

The angrier I became the bigger my hair got. Soon I was huffing and puffing until I wondered if steam would start coming out of my ears! All of a sudden, the Lord spoke to me. He said, "You really look silly."

I thought, "Yeah, I do." But He didn't mean my hair. He meant my spiritual condition. He reminded me that I needed to think about what I'd been thinking about. Most of our "battles" begin in the mind. He showed me that we often try to battle thoughts with thoughts, but we're supposed to fight thoughts with words — decisive words.

When the tempter came against Jesus, He countered everything Satan said with Scripture, *...It is written...* (Matthew 4:4). When the devil comes against your mind, you need to speak the Word of God, and that's what I had

to do about that person who had said something unkind and untrue about me. I needed to *decide* to forgive, walk in love, speak the Word over her, and pray for her.

You are reading this book because you have chosen to take the necessary steps to overcome intimidation, fear, and insecurity, and make quality decisions that will cause you to rise above your circumstances, the past, and the lies of the enemy of your soul. And you can do it! Your faith is making you strong!

Most of our "battles"
begin in the mind.
God showed me that we
often try to battle thoughts
with thoughts, but we're
supposed to fight thoughts
with words —
decisive words.

Chapter Five

FREE FROM THE POWER OF REJECTION

FREE FROM THE POWER OF REJECTION

He is despised and rejected of men....

— Isaiah 53:3

Isaiah 53:3 reminds us that Jesus experienced rejection so that we could experience victory over it! Isaiah lets us know that Jesus was a man so familiar with rejection during His life on earth that He came to *understand* sorrow and pain. But, like Jesus, we have been given the supernatural ability to overcome rejection and live in freedom!

Webster's Dictionary defines the word *rejection* as "to refuse to accept, recognize, or make use of; to throw away, or discard." Rejection begins with a seed planted — often at a very early age — and sometimes by those who should care most about us. Yes, rejection wounds our emotions and yet we have to keep in mind that as born-again believers, the Holy Spirit lives in us to strengthen and comfort us.

My personal experience with rejection set the pace for some very uncomfortable growing up years. Feeling as though no one really liked me because I had been "tagged" a slow learner and sent to special education classes beginning with fifth grade, I was the brunt of such painful teasing that I developed an overwhelming inferiority complex.

"What's Wrong with Me?"

At one point I even wondered if I was mentally retarded, and asked my sister, Helen, to tell me what was wrong with me. I had decided that my family and friends were withholding this information from me because they couldn't stand to cause me even more pain than I was already experiencing at school. The devil is so mean!

I grew to *expect* rejection from people. And all of my expectations were met! In a mock election held at my high school to determine each student's yearbook slogan, even though I expected the best slogans to go to the popular kids, I didn't expect the devastating results of the election for myself. I was actually voted "Least Likely to Succeed" out of my class of more than six hundred! I went home and ran to my bedroom sobbing. I blurted out to God: "If You don't do something fast, I'm going to kill myself!"

God was already in the process of doing something, but I was too discouraged and ignorant of spiritual things to realize it. Through a series of events taking place behind the scenes, my cousin, a born-again, Spirit-filled graduate of Rhema Bible Training Center in Tulsa, Oklahoma, shared the Gospel with my mother. She had suffered for eight years with chronic back pain, and after visiting with my cousin, decided to fly to Oklahoma to attend Rhema's Healing School.

While Mom was there, she was baptized in the Holy Spirit and learned the biblical principles she needed to stand in faith for her healing. When she came home, she fed her spirit on Brother Hagin's books and tapes and applied the faith principles to her physical condition. Nine months later, she woke up completely healed! This miracle of healing became the divine catalyst for my miracle of transformation. I'll talk more about that in this and upcoming chapters.

Many people suffer from the hurtful fruits of rejection, and without faith in God and His power to heal and deliver, the inevitable result is unproductive, frustrating lives filled with the pain of insecurity. I believe Satan works overtime on his powerful weapon of rejection because he knows it has the ability to paralyze and immobilize us to inaction. And as Christians we then will be of little or no effect, and that's exactly what the devil wants.

We can become so intimidated that it seems as though there must be something so terribly wrong with us that we develop the idea that we're unacceptable and unsuitable for anyone or anything. We actually reject ourselves because someone else rejected us!

To battle and overcome these negative thoughts, we must recognize and be sure of their source. John 10:10 confirms that it is the thief (Satan) who comes only to steal, kill and destroy us, and that Jesus came to give us abundant life. It is very clear, then, that God is not the author of turmoil and the creator of rejection, but that thieving devil is responsible. Once this fact is established, we have to prepare ourselves to fight the good fight of faith!

God had great plans for my life, and it began when my mother received the Lord and was healed of several physical conditions. She immediately began to share the goodness and love of God with me. I was sixteen years old.

Within a matter of weeks, Kenneth E. Hagin came to my hometown of Detroit, Michigan, to hold a crusade. My mother, my aunt, several cousins, and I attended the crusade the first night, and when Brother Hagin gave the altar call, although I knew I needed to be saved, I didn't go forward. I was embarrassed (just another form of intimidation) because my cousins were there.

Brother Hagin's prayer at the conclusion of the altar call kept me awake throughout a very long night. He prayed, "Lord, if there is anyone here who doesn't know You as Savior, I pray that they won't be able to eat or sleep or find any rest until they make You the Lord of their life." I knew I had to get back there again.

The next night when the altar call came, I went forward with scores of other people who had a desire to be saved and confessed Jesus Christ as my Lord and Savior. Afterward, Brother Hagin laid hands on me to be filled with the Holy Spirit. And when he did, the power of God hit me, and I began speaking in other tongues. I felt as if a great burden was lifted off my shoulders. Depression and fear that had oppressed me for so long was gone! I had heard the truth — and in one life-changing moment, the truth had set me free!

God Loves Me!

As I began to study the Word of God, I realized that He loved me as His own beloved child. My heavenly Father's love, abundant blessing, and divine favor had been poured out on me! I discovered that God believed only good things about me. He knew that He had blessed me with gifts, talents, and abilities uniquely my own, and He knew that He would call me to preach and teach His Word. God thought I had potential! And I began to defeat the devil's lies with the truth of God's Word about me.

Remember how much I loved to play basketball at home with my brothers? Well, the coach hardly ever let me play in school-sponsored games because I was so timid and made so many mistakes. But once I learned that I was entitled to walk in God's supernatural favor as His own daughter, I stopped seeing myself as the rejected Kate and saw myself walking hand-in-hand with Father God. I made a conscious decision to see myself the way God sees me.

My faith worked! I was no longer timid and shy with my coach and the members of the basketball team. I had become a brand-new person! Just about everyone I knew was shocked that the once shy, timid Kate had been transformed into one of the top basketball players on that high school's team.

The Kate who hadn't been able to give an oral book report without thinking I would faint was now preaching the Gospel! Classmates looked to me as a spiritual leader, and I led many of them to Christ as they witnessed the dramatic changes in my life.

I am living proof that in Christ we are more than conquerors. Romans 8:37 says, *...in all these things* [including intimidating rejection and its debilitating effects] *we are more than conquerors through him that loved us.* We must have faith, believe God's Word is true, and act on it.

Somebody's Gonna Get Saved!

I didn't know one Christian when I began my junior year in high school, so I decided to make some Christians myself by preaching the Gospel and getting people saved! I reversed the peer-pressure principle. If someone asked me, "Do you actually go to church?" I'd answer, "You mean, you don't? What's wrong with you? You aren't filled with the Holy Spirit? You don't speak in other tongues? Man, you're strange! I'm the one who is normal!"

I grew uncharacteristically bold! But my unorthodox approach worked with many of my peers, and several of them came to the Lord throughout the school year, including some teammates on the basketball team.

I looked for opportunities to preach or share my testimony wherever I could — the local Rescue Mission, at Bible studies, and at youth groups. God's Word was my lifeline, as necessary as the air I breathed. The contrast between the misery and hopelessness I had lived with for years and the freedom and joy I now experienced was immense.

Normal teenage activities held no fascination for me. Every day I spent hours studying the Word, reading Brother Hagin's books, listening to his tapes, and fellowshipping with the Lord in prayer.

With special education classes behind me, I took my place in regular classes during my junior year due to the supernatural changes that had taken place in my life. And with God, I made excellent grades during my last year of high school, enjoyed record-breaking achievements on the basketball court (my team took first place in our conference!), and the blessing of an abundance of friends who liked and respected me.

I am here to tell you that God loves you. He wants you to be happy, and He wants you to succeed. When you *expect* to be mistreated and rejected by others, that will surely happen. But when you know who you are in Christ and realize that He cares about everything that concerns you, you will learn to *expect* God's divine favor to go to work on your behalf.

God wants to see you step out and exercise all the power He has already provided for you to conquer intimidating fear and rejection. Trust in Him, and you can rise above the effects of rejection and begin to produce lasting fruit for the Kingdom.

Stepping Out in Faith

Within weeks of my conversion, I was given an unexpected opportunity to "step into the waters" of my divine call for a trial run. Someone who had heard my testimony invited me to preach at a drug rehabilitation center chapel service. I accepted the invitation, not realizing that my first "congregation" would be around four hundred drug addicts and alcoholics who were required to attend chapel if they wanted to eat!

I had absolutely no idea what I was going to say! I prayed in the Holy Ghost throughout the day before, trying to figure out a sermon, but I couldn't think of anything! Finally, I prayed, "Lord, You know how I was not too long ago. I was so scared, I couldn't stand to think about talking in front of people. With Your help, Lord, I know I can share the Gospel with these people. Thank You for anointing me to preach to them."

I walked up to the pulpit silently praying, "Lord, what do I tell them?" Suddenly the Lord spoke to my heart: "Just tell them what you know." I thought, *Oh, that's good! I know two things: God is a good God because He set me free. And anyone that doesn't serve Him is just dumb!*

For forty-five minutes, I walked around declaring the simple message that God is a good God — and that not serving Him was dumb! I was sure the businessman who had invited me was sitting there thinking, *Oh, no, I missed God when I asked this girl to preach!*

At the conclusion of the service, I asked the entire audience to stand. I said, "I invite you to receive this good God. You can be saved, healed, filled with the Holy Ghost, and delivered! And those of you who want to be dumb and go to hell, just go ahead and sit down!"

Nobody sat down! More than four hundred drug addicts and alcoholics came forward that night to receive Jesus, weeping in repentance before the Lord! Praise God!

(Perhaps you have come to the realization that God has gifted you in a certain area that would be a blessing to others, but you haven't stepped out in faith and even "tested the waters" for fear of being rejected.)

Remember that the Greater One lives in you, and He is waiting for you to allow Him to be your strength today and every day! *Praise God*

Praying to God or Man?

I have found that people are often uncomfortable about praying in front of other people. Have you ever felt a little intimidated around those who seem to pray beautiful prayers with lots of flowery words? You start thinking, *They can pray me under the chair! Dear God, don't let anybody call on me to pray!*

I've experienced this myself among other ministers. With all of the knowledge I'd acquired from the Word, I was still intimidated about praying with people who I deemed as great men and women of God. Whenever I was in that situation, I found myself actually praying to impress them. Of course, I knew better than to do that, and yet here I was allowing myself to get all tuned up to impress men!

I thank God that He won't let me get far out of line. Right away He said, "Kate, what are you doing? Who are you trying to impress? Certainly not Me. All your flowery phrases and impassioned pleas won't get you anywhere with Me." You see, I was more conscious of what they were hearing than what God was hearing. Don't worry about how you sound to people. You're not praying to them anyway.

My ministry staff gathers each week to pray for our partners. During this time, we also pray about specific ministry needs, different people's personal and professional needs, and we pray over the prayer requests that come into the office by mail and phone. Different staff members take turns praying, and I can easily tell by the facial expressions and body language that some staff members are more reluctant than others to pray before the whole group.

Some have even said, "I wish no one would ask me because I can't pray as well as they do." I certainly don't want them to be so worried that I will ask them to pray that they can't even focus on our prayer and be in agreement with it, but I also refuse to participate in the devil's plan to

hinder their prayer lives. I remind them that God is not looking at how we pray. He looks at the heart.

God's not listening to how beautifully your words are phrased, but He is concerned if you're praying to be heard of other people and how you sound to them. That's not the right motive for prayer — prayer is conversation with God. We're supposed to be talking with Him.

We have to purpose in our hearts that we are going to do whatever it is that God has called us to do, and we will not allow the devil to rob us. We are not going to be intimidated, but we're going to be bold and become all that God has called us to be.

Willingness and obedience to do whatever God directs us to do is one of the keys to our victory over rejection and intimidation, but we must be committed to God and to His Word.

You don't have to receive rejection. Rejection can be a deep-seated issue, and working hand-in-hand with God will result in your healing. God is faithful, and faith in Him and the truth of His Word produces boldness in us. You are an overcomer! The Bible says, *Fight the good fight of faith, lay hold on eternal life, whereunto thou art also called, and hast professed a good profession before many witnesses* (1 Timothy 6:12).

The Power of Our Own Words

The words of our mouth need to line up with God's Word. How we feel about ourselves can quickly be picked up by the way we speak about others and ourselves. We should avoid saying negative things about ourselves such as, "I can't do anything right," "This is just the way I am, and I will never change," "I look awful," or "I'm just stupid." Remember Proverbs 23:7, *For as he thinketh in his heart, so is he....*

Speak good things to yourself about yourself. God's Word says great things about you. Believe them! Stand in front of a mirror and declare that you are a servant of God, acceptable to Him, and approved of men (see Romans 14:18). Say to yourself, "I am not a mistake. God loves me. He's happy with me. He has a good plan for my life. He thinks wonderful things about me, and they're all true! By faith I will fulfill my purpose on earth."

Say, "I am created in the likeness of Christ Jesus, my Lord and my Savior. My Creator designed me for a wonderful purpose. As a partaker of His divine nature, I will positively respond to God's call on my life. Jesus loves me, this I know, for the Bible tells me so!"

Concentrate on Your Strengths — Not Your Weaknesses

As a blood-bought child of God, you don't have to allow old patterns and negative circumstances to affect your walk with the Lord. You have a choice — you can choose to be either positive or negative, but negative people seldom allow themselves to enjoy life, and they are certainly not fun to be with.

They often exercise the facial muscles around their mouth by complaining, criticizing, and finding fault with everything and everyone to anyone who'll listen. If this has been a weakness of yours, you can turn it into strength with your own mouth. And when you start thinking positive thoughts and saying positive words about yourself and others, good things are going to happen to you.

When you seek the Lord first and abide in Him, He will impart all the power you need to manifest your strengths and not your weaknesses. When you confess these words and really mean them deep down in your heart, I believe you will be amazed at the changes that will take place in your life.

Transformed into His Image

God searches for those who are willing to let go of the harmful effects of rejection and fear and be changed into what He alone can make them. Every child of God can be transformed into the very image of Christ Jesus according to 2 Corinthians 3:18 AMP, *And all of us, as with unveiled face, [because we] continued to behold [in the Word of God] as in a mirror the glory of the Lord, are constantly being transfigured into His very own image in ever increasing splendor and from one degree of glory to another; [for this comes] from the Lord [Who is] the Spirit.*

Every aspect of our lives is affected by what we believe. When we believe the truth of God's Word, our minds are renewed. Romans 12:2 says, *And be not conformed to this world: but be ye transformed by the renewing of your mind, that ye may prove what is that good, and acceptable, and perfect, will of God.* Then we can experience God's perfect plan for our lives. We will not get beyond our own opinion of ourselves until we believe what God says about us.

I encourage you to take an inventory of the issues you are facing and deal with them. If the pain of rejection has hindered your walk with God and His call on your life, remember that you don't have to be perfect in order to receive His acceptance, help, and love. He is on your side! He wants you to like yourself — to be your own best friend. When you cooperate with God's plan for your life, you will begin to see yourself as a valuable, necessary part of the body of Christ — without which the Body is incomplete.

When you really know who you are in Christ, you don't have to spend your time trying to prove your worth. You can experience for yourself the peace and contentment that comes from God alone. He loves you so much that He gave His own life to conquer intimidation and rejection once and for all! Through your faith in Jesus Christ, you can be secure in who you are as an individual — regardless of your station in life.

Accepted in the Beloved

God doesn't look at you according to how much money you have or don't have, how intelligent you are or are not, your level of education, your family's position in the community, or whatever criteria the world sets as a standard of acceptability. You are accepted in the beloved according to Ephesians 1:6.

Nobody is perfect, including those who you feel have rejected, hurt, and disappointed you. I urge you to take each of your festering wounds to Jesus, lay them at His feet, and start receiving His healing grace. Cast all your wounds on Him and leave them there. Don't pick them up again. Don't use your mouth to discuss them with another person, and don't allow them to play like a recording over and over in your mind.

Leave your wounds at Jesus' feet. He knows all about being wounded and is far more able to handle your situation than you are. Claim Jeremiah 30:17 as your special-delivery promise from the Lord: *For I will restore health unto thee, and I will heal thee of thy wounds, saith the Lord; because they called thee an Outcast, saying, This is Zion, whom no man seeketh after.*

Miracles Come in "Cans"

If you feel "under attack" right now, and the devil is telling you that you are not able to overcome it, I want you to know that I believe you can. I always say that miracles come in cans — "God *can*, Jesus *can*, the Holy Ghost *can*, and I *can*." Please believe me when I say that I am completely free from the devastating effects of rejection. And since God is no respecter of persons (see Acts 10:34), I know He'll do the same thing for you.

I encourage you to commit yourself to spend quality time in God's presence, stay strong in the power of His might, and prepare yourself to start enjoying your life. It's not too late. You *can* have peace in the midst of your storm — today.

When you *expect* to be mistreated and rejected by others, that will surely happen. But when you know who you are in Christ and realize that He cares about everything that concerns you, you will learn to *expect* God's divine favor to go to work on your behalf.

Chapter Six

SECURITY IN GOD IS SO GOOD

SECURITY IN GOD IS SO GOOD

The Lord is my light and my salvation; whom shall I fear? the Lord is the strength of my life; of whom shall I be afraid?

— Psalm 27:1

Notice that John 14:27 in The Amplified Bible actually states, ...*do not permit yourselves to be fearful and intimidated....* You have to do it by not allowing yourself to be intimidated.

If you have been ministered to so far in this book, I encourage you again to never allow the devil to rob you of *any* blessing. If you're insecure about going to church because you don't have anyone to go with, gather up the courage God gave you and be secure enough to get up and go. Walk through the doors with your head held high and say to yourself, "I refuse to allow myself to be intimidated. I refuse to be robbed of the blessing of fellowship with the saints!"

When I first started traveling years ago, I traveled by myself because I didn't have the money to pay anyone to accompany me. I went to all kinds of places to minister alone. I flew halfway around the world to places I'd never been.

I was once on the same flight with another Bible teacher. It appeared that she, too, was traveling alone, so I asked, "Are you all by yourself?" And she said, "Oh no, I have a whole bunch of people with me." Right away, I started thinking, *She has a whole staff of people with her. She doesn't have to travel all alone.* But when we got aboard, I noticed that she was still by herself. I thought, *Nobody's with her. I'm going to talk to her.*

I said, "I thought you were flying with a whole bunch of people." She said, "Yes, a bunch of folks." I asked her where they were because I hadn't noticed any of them. She said, "All of my angels, God, the Holy Ghost, and Jesus. They're all here with me." I felt so silly. Supposedly, I was a spiritual preacher — and I hadn't figured out what she was talking about.

After that, when people asked me, "You're going to go to those meetings all alone?" I'd say, "No, I'm going with God, Jesus, and the Holy Ghost." But in the natural, I was by myself. I'd get off the plane, and start looking for the person who had been sent to meet me. I usually hadn't met them before, and I sometimes felt a little intimidated. I'd start thinking, "Okay, who is it? Where am I going?"

I'd look for someone who *looked* like a Christian. I would smile and look for the *glow*. If someone smiled back, they might be from the church where I was supposed to preach. If nobody smiled back, I'd just stand there feeling awkward. I had to learn to be secure in who I am in God.

The safest place to be is in the will of God. It doesn't matter if He sends you to the Philippines or to Russia...or if He sends you right into the middle of a war. If that's His will, you're in the safest place there is — even in an airplane.

Fear of Flying

I once had a genuine fear of flying. I never told anyone about this, and for quite some time, nobody seemed to notice that I drove almost everywhere that I was going to preach. Obviously, I couldn't continue to avoid flying and get to meetings on time, so eventually I had to fly. That's when the real battle with fear escalated.

I determined that I was not going to let the devil intimidate me into immobility, so I just flew all over the country — afraid. During that time, the devil kept at me constantly. I'd hear a little noise, and my heart would start pounding. Later I'd discover that it was the landing gear that made the particular noise that always set me on edge. Fear is cruel and horrible!

One time the pilot came on the speaker system and said he had some really bad news. My heart sank! All kinds of terrible things filtered through my brain until he said, "We're out of coffee!"

I've been on planes that were met by sirens screaming from fire trucks and lots of activity out on the runway, obviously waiting for the plane that I was on! You think, "Oh, what's wrong? That's my plane they're in a frenzy about. Why are they waiting for my plane? Is there a bomb?"

But the fact is that I know I'm safe in the perfect will of God, and I have angels. I don't have to worry about anything, and neither do you. I learned that by searching out every single scripture I could locate on angels, protection, and overcoming fear. I started studying the blood of Jesus, and I'd speak and confess these scriptures over myself.

All of this study and confession proved very beneficial when I was on a plane that flew into a bad thunderstorm and dropped one thousand feet of altitude. People were screaming. Everybody's food and drinks hit the ceiling. There was debris flying everywhere! I was soaked because my soft drink hit the ceiling and came splashing down all over me. Immediately the devil started in with his old news about the plane falling out of the sky, but I was prepared this time.

God actually gave me a poem while all of this was going on, and I wrote it down. Some of the greatest things you get from God are sometimes right in the midst of some of your most challenging times. This is what I wrote:

No fear lives here,

No fear lives here,

I will not let it in,

Although it comes knocking, time and time again.

"What will you do?" fear says to you,

But don't you give it place.

God's angels protect me from evil against me,

I'm covered by His grace.

So when the feelings of fear arise,

And the devil speaks his lies,

Be bold and full of faith,

I'm covered and protected by the blood, in Jesus' name.

So no matter where I go,

By land, or sea, or plane,

My angels — they go with me,

I will not fear again.

The Lord set me free to such a degree that when a very gracious person offered to fly me in her airplane to my meetings, I accepted because I was not going to let the devil rip me off anymore. I actually went from being afraid of flying to landing an airplane myself! And I am totally delivered to this day! You can be free from fear too!

We need to be secure in who we are in God, and we need to be confident and enjoy life. Too many people miss out on things that they would really enjoy because they're intimidated. They won't go and do things because they're intimidated. Some won't even go to church because they feel that their clothes are not nice enough. The secret to being secure is knowing who you are in Christ — not in what you wear.

Eating Out Alone

There are people who wouldn't consider eating out at a restaurant alone. I didn't think I could do it either at one time, although I obviously had to when I started traveling alone to minister at different places. It was just another intimidation-based issue.

I used to tease a minister friend of mine who regularly ate out alone. I'd call her on her cell phone and ask what she was doing. She would respond that she was eating out in a nice restaurant.

I'd always ask who she was with, and she usually said, "Nobody." She wasn't intimidated in the least. I'd say, "You're only doing that because you don't have any friends." That was mean, wasn't it? And, of course, that wasn't the case at all. But it did prompt me to wonder whether I was as secure as she was. So I tested myself to see how I'd react.

I went to a nice restaurant, and sure enough, intimidation was right there. I *thought* people were looking strangely at me because I was by myself. I *supposed* they felt sorry for me because I must not have any friends — the very thing I'd innocently teased my friend about. But then something wonderful happened. The Holy Ghost reminded me that all these people were out to enjoy a nice meal at this restaurant, and I was not what was on their minds! We are not on other people's minds as much as we think we are.

Nobody was really looking at me strangely at all. I *imagined* all that with a little help from the devil. Right then and there, I cast down that imagination and enjoyed myself while I had a nice dinner. I can eat out alone if I choose to, without the companionship of my old friends — insecurity and intimidation. And I can honestly say that I don't give a thought to what anybody thinks about it.

Are Your "Who" and Your "Do" Mixed Up?

I heard one minister say that our security should be in who we are in Christ, but many times, it stems from what we do, our level of education, our family tree, or the brand name on our clothes. Our "who" and our "do" are all mixed up!

Many people think if they worked in a certain profession or held a lofty position, they'd be secure because everybody would like them and recognize their worth and value. We don't value individuals for who they are in this society of the nuclear age — the worth of people is placed on what they *do*. We don't ask *who* they are when we see someone we've never met. We ask, "What do you *do?*" We seldom ask how people *are* any more. We ask, "How are you *doing?*" This thinking pattern isn't easy to shake off in this day and age.

Acceptance of ourselves has to be kept separate from what we do. We can be secure simply because Jesus Christ lives on the inside of us. God made us who we are, and therefore we can be secure because we're in Christ. Every now and then I think: *God would love me just as much whether or not I ever preached the Gospel again. He'd still bless me because my relationship with Him isn't as a preacher talking to God. It's me talking to God — fellowshipping with my Father.*

God doesn't love you more when you have a certain position or because you *do* something for Him. He loves you for *who* you are. And He doesn't love you less when you've messed up. God doesn't want you to continually carry around a load of guilt because you've made mistakes. Everybody makes those! You haven't cornered the market on making mistakes.

The good news is that Jesus paid the price for our mistakes when He died on the cross. When He conquered death with His resurrection, we were completely set free from the bondage of sin, and that's how God sees us now. He has created a way for our mistakes to be paid in full by the sacrifice of His Son, our Savior, Jesus Christ. Hallelujah!

Guilt and Forgiving Yourself

Insecure people have a hard time forgiving themselves and moving on. If you're dealing with the guilt of past mistakes, I believe this is the time to finally put it in the past.

I remember a minister talking about feeling guilty over something he had done wrong. All day long, he was miserable because of what seemed to him to be a terrible failure. I used to think like that. The bigger the sin in my own mind, the longer it took for me to get over the guilt. If the sin didn't seem as significant to me, then I only felt guilty for a little while.

I once heard a preacher say that he had really been "beating himself up" over something when suddenly he heard the Holy Spirit say, "I forgave you the instant you asked Me to. When do you plan on forgiving yourself? Haven't you been dragging that guilt around long enough?" Wow! What a revelation!

I had experienced that myself. I had asked the Lord to forgive me, but I kept holding on to it. Have you found out that when you don't forgive yourself — when you don't act on the Word of God — your prayer life is hindered? You cannot boldly enter the throne room of God when you're feeling guilty.

The sooner you act on the Word and forgive yourself, the better it will be for you and for all those around you. You cannot effectively minister to other people if you're holding on to guilt. You have to purpose in your heart that you're going to forgive and love yourself.

Pray for Boldness

Insecure people often shrink back and let other people dominate or overpower them, but instead, they should pray for boldness. Acts 4:24, 29, and 31 describes what happened as a result of this type of prayer. The apostles Peter and John had been arrested and instructed to never again teach about or in the name of Jesus. When they were released, they gathered with other believers and prayed. They said, …*Lord, thou art God, which hast made heaven, and earth, and the sea, and all that in them is.* …*Lord, behold their threatenings: and grant unto thy servants, that with all boldness they may speak thy word.* Verse 31 says that …*when they had prayed, the place was shaken where they were assembled together; and they were all*

filled with the Holy Ghost, and they spake the word of God with boldness.

Proverbs 28:1 says, *...the righteous are bold as a lion.* It is scriptural to pray for boldness. I pray for boldness in preaching all the time. And if you pray for ministers, I encourage you to ask God to give them boldness — that they'll boldly open their mouths and say what God puts in their heart.

We have to be bold when we speak for Jesus. If I were to try to minister with a weak, shaky voice and say something like, "I h-h-h-have some things to sh-sh-shhare with you and m-m-m-maybe God can s-s-s-somehow b-b-b-bless you with this m-m-message," it would be hard to believe and receive.

You can boldly proclaim the Word of God and remain humble in your heart toward the Lord. There is a difference between boldness and arrogance. Boldly speaking the Word doesn't mean you're in pride.

I think people sometimes mistake boldness for rudeness, and that may be the case with some folks, but not always. The subject of boldness becomes touchy when it is misinterpreted as a license to be pushy or domineering. I am certainly not suggesting that anyone pray for boldness so they can walk all over everybody. We don't need that spirit to get into the Church!

Nothing to Prove

Many women ministers may feel like they have to prove that they are called. But they don't have to prove anything. There's an old saying that goes something like this: "The proof of the pudding is in the eating."

I don't have to prove anything to anybody. Why? Because I'm confident in who God called me to be and in what He called me to do. I know that God will make the way for me — He has already done it in countless ways. I believe He will continue to open wide doors of opportunity for me to minister, and I don't have to be pushy. I speak the truth in love, follow the precepts laid out in the Word of God, and trust God to do the rest.

I believe people really want to be ministered to — they want the truth. They aren't as interested in the messenger as they are the message. They like a "straight shooter" so to speak. I know that I do. Some of my favorite preachers are very bold. They can step on my toes until they almost fall off! Personally, I grow under that kind of preaching.

When somebody puts it to you plainly — "Listen, you need to straighten up in this area" — Bam! In my spirit, I say, "Thank you, I needed that." I feel as though God has come down and spoken to me personally! It's glorious!

My flesh isn't always comfortable, but my spirit man likes it when someone ministers truth and makes it easy to understand. I've heard people say something as simple as, "If you're not speaking the Word, doing the Word, and meditating on the Word — you're missing it." It's simple, but when you think about it, many times that is where we're missing it.

Believe That You Receive

What's wrong with acting as you would if you were a secure person? You are secure in God. In other words, believe you receive confidence by faith as you would receive everything else in your life by faith. Start acting like you are a secure person by faith. When you come up against an intimidating situation, ask yourself, "How would I act if I were secure?"

Even though you don't feel like it, your feelings will eventually line up. I remember when the Lord prompted me to sing more when I ministered at different churches. I didn't like singing — especially in churches that had the best singers you ever heard. And some had huge orchestras! Here I was in front of this great orchestra, and all of a sudden my knees would start knocking.

I'd be about to open my mouth when the devil would start in, "You never sang with a big orchestra before…in a huge church like this…with all these great singers. They're professionals. Who are you?"

And here it came: Intimidation! I knew immediately what I had to do. I had to take those negative thoughts captive and decide to act as I would if I were a confident singer! I acted as though I sang with a great group of folks like these every day of my life.

Now it's important to be realistic about your strengths and weaknesses. I am not really a singer per se, but the Lord does give me choruses. And I can teach them to others who can sing, and they are blessed. Sometimes we just need to have that childlike faith.

Kids Don't Care

You can stand a child up in front of a thousand people, and though some are timid and shy, there are those who would grab the microphone and sing a song totally off key and not really care at all! We adults might want to take some lessons from children. Adults have all kinds of fears, but children don't worry about anything.

Recently, a friend and I were talking about fearful people — particularly those who are afraid of driving a car. They get in the car and buckle up their seat belt (which we all need to do, of course), but they're nervous — pretty sure that if something is going to happen, it will happen to them. They're nervous about traffic. They're really nervous if there are kids in the car.

But for the kids, it's entirely different. They're already playing a game before you can shut the door. They aren't nervous. They're sure that they are going to arrive at their destination. In fact, they don't give it a thought. They're not concerned. They aren't worried. Why? They trust their parents, grandparents, the school bus driver, or whoever is driving the car.

We need to trust our heavenly Father this same way, knowing that He's able to take care of us. We *can* have victory over insecurity, intimidation, rejection, and anxiety in our lives. You can be set free to enjoy great peace in God when you trust Him to keep you safely under His wing.

Start acting like
you are a secure person
by faith.
When you come up against
an intimidating situation,
ask yourself,
"How would I act if
I were secure?"

Chapter Seven

TEN WAYS TO OVERCOME

TEN WAYS TO OVERCOME

Be careful for nothing; but in every thing by prayer and supplication with thanksgiving let your requests be made known unto God.

— Philippians 4:6

When you've been in an insecure situation and then experienced a situation where you felt secure, you know how much better it feels to be secure. We've discussed fear, intimidation, anxiety, and rejection in the previous chapters. Now I want to focus on ten ways you can overcome these peace-stealers.

Remember that I experienced these things myself, but once I accepted Jesus, I began to put the Word to work in my life. I confessed scriptures over myself until I believed what God said about me rather than the devil's lies about me.

The results were astounding! I was miraculously healed and transformed by the power of God! Many people have asked me how I overcame and that's what I'm going to share in this chapter.

#1 — Faith Talk

I was really blessed when the Lord gave me this instruction to start speaking a new language He called "Faith Talk." He led me to look up scriptures that are uplifting and encouraging — scriptures that remind you of who you are in Christ and minister boldness and encouragement in your life. I believe that if you begin confessing and personalizing these scriptures to your own life and situations, you, too, will reap the rewards of a miraculous transformation. I encourage you to compile an assortment of positive things that you can say about yourself that will minister to you:

Peace I leave with you; My [own] peace I now give and

bequeath to you. Not as the world gives do I give to

you. Do not let your hearts be troubled, neither let

them be afraid. [Stop allowing yourselves to be agitated

and disturbed; and do not permit yourselves to be fear-

ful and intimidated and cowardly and unsettled.]

— John 14:27 AMP

To personalize this scripture to your own life, your confession of faith will be something like this:

("God's Word says that Jesus left me His peace. I have His own peace because He bequeathed it to me. It's not the kind of peace the world gives. I will not let my heart be troubled, neither will I let it be afraid. I will not allow myself to be agitated and disturbed, and I will not permit myself to be fearful, intimidated, cowardly, and unsettled.")

Isn't that edifying and uplifting to your spirit? It is to mine!

I have strength for all things in Christ Who empow-

ers me [I am ready for anything and equal to any-

thing through Him Who infuses inner strength into

me; I am self-sufficient in Christ's sufficiency].

— Philippians 4:13 AMP

This one is already written in an applicable way to our personal lives. I love Colossians 1:8-14 from The Amplified Bible:

> Also he has informed us of your love in the [Holy] Spirit. For this reason we also, from the day we heard of it, have not ceased to pray and make [special] request for you, [asking] that you may be filled with the full (deep and clear) knowledge of His will in all spiritual wisdom [in comprehensive insight into the ways and purposes of God] and in understanding and discernment of spiritual things — that you may walk (live and conduct yourselves) in a manner worthy of the Lord, fully pleasing to Him and desiring to please Him in all things, bearing fruit in every good work and steadily growing and increasing in and by the knowledge of God [with fuller, deeper, and clearer insight, acquaintance, and recognition]. [We pray] that you may be invigorated and strengthened with all power according to the might of His glory, [to exercise] every kind of endurance and patience (perseverance and forbearance) with joy, giving thanks to the Father, Who has qualified and made us fit to share the portion which

is the inheritance of the saints (God's holy people) in
the Light. [The Father] has delivered and drawn us
to Himself out of the control and the dominion of
darkness and has transferred us into the kingdom of
the Son of His love, in Whom we have our redemp-
tion through His blood, [which means] the forgive-
ness of our sins.

Repeat these verses to yourself something like this:

"I love people in the Holy Spirit. I am not afraid of
them. I thank God that I am filled with the full, deep, and
clear knowledge of His will in all spiritual wisdom with insight
into His ways and purposes, and I have understanding and dis-
cernment of spiritual things. I walk, live, and conduct myself
in a manner worthy of my Lord and Savior, Jesus Christ, fully
pleasing Him and desiring to please Him in all things.

"I bear fruit in every good work and steadily grow and
increase in and by the knowledge of God with fuller, deeper,
and clearer insight, acquaintance, and recognition. I am
invigorated and strengthened with all power according to the
might of His glory, to exercise every kind of endurance,
patience, perseverance, and forbearance with joy.

"I give thanks to the Father, Who has qualified and
made me fit to share the portion which is the inheritance of

the saints (that's me — one of God's holy people) in the Light. Father God has delivered me out of darkness and into the kingdom of the Son of His love. My sins are forgiven, and my life has been redeemed by the blood of Jesus."

Isn't it wonderful to dig these treasures out of God's Word and apply them to yourself? I love it. I think you get the idea of how to do this now, so I will focus only on the scriptures that have been especially helpful to me with regard to intimidation, insecurity, rejection, and anxiety. You know how to paraphrase them for yourself:

In the reverent and worshipful fear of the Lord there is strong confidence, and His children shall always have a place of refuge.

— Proverbs 14:26 AMP

For the Lord shall be your confidence, firm and strong, and shall keep your foot from being caught [in a trap or some hidden danger].

— Proverbs 3:26 AMP

It is better to trust and take refuge in the Lord than to put confidence in man.

— Psalm 118:8 AMP

And they shall dwell safely in [their own land] and shall build houses and plant vineyards; yes, they shall dwell securely and with confidence when I have executed judgments and punishments upon all those round about them who have despised and trodden upon them and pushed them away, and they shall know (understand and realize) that I am the Lord their God [their Sovereign Ruler, Who calls forth loyalty and obedient service].

— Ezekiel 28:26 AMP

Paul...welcomed all who came to him, preaching to them the kingdom of God and teaching them about the Lord Jesus Christ with boldness and quite openly, and without being molested or hindered.

— Acts 28:30,31 AMP

And this is the confidence (the assurance, the privilege of boldness) which we have in Him: [we are sure] that if we ask anything (make any request) according to His will (in agreement with His own plan), He listens to and hears us.

— 1 John 5:14 AMP

#2 — Don't Talk about the Problem

Faith talk doesn't bemoan the issues of fear and insecurity. Once faith gets down deep inside you, you won't want to use your mouth to claim that you still have a problem with those old issues. But it is good to keep reminding ourselves that we're now faith people. We know God has given us the weapons we need to combat those negative thoughts, but sometimes that's not easy — especially if you've been talking negatively for a long time. It may take some time to exchange all your negatives for positives.

You can really get ahead of the devil if you keep your thoughts and conversation focused on good things and the ways in which you are noticing changes for the better in yourself.

Remember, God is good and the devil is bad. Satan will try to throw obstacles in your path to thwart your progress, but don't let him! You have the mind of Christ. Your positive words about yourself and others can release physical energy and healing.

I believe the Holy Spirit is grieved when we speak negatively about ourselves. After all, He is our Creator. We were created in His own likeness. His ways and thoughts, which are higher than ours according to Isaiah 55:9, are not negative toward us.

Have you ever thought about this? When you speak negatively about yourself, you imply that God didn't do His best when He made you. How do you feel when people say unkind things about your work?

#3 — Forgive...and Leave the Past in the Past

Focusing on the past is unfruitful. It's best to leave the past in the past. Yes, it is painful to be the object of people's abuse — unkind jokes, finger-pointing, and insensitivity — but forgiveness has an important part to play in overcoming intimidation and insecurity.

So many people waste their entire lives hating those who caused them pain, and it is highly likely that those people aren't even aware of what they've done. They've gone on with their lives, while a "victim mentality" has moved in and made a home in the heart of the one who was injured.

Keeping a list of the "sins" perpetrated on us at the hands of another can so occupy our minds that it becomes difficult to accomplish anything. Again, we are paralyzed into inactivity. Don't waste your present and your future worrying about the past. I like what one minister says,

"Learn from your past and prepare for your future, but live in the present!"

When you have been hurt, rejected, or offended, it's natural to feel wounded and misunderstood, or you may feel resentful and angry toward that person. But regardless of how you feel, you will fall into the trap the devil has set for you if you don't make the decision to let it go.

God wants to set you free from the hurts of the past. No matter what you've done, the word *past* means "past." The Bible says it is God *Who forgiveth all thine iniquities; who healeth all thy diseases* (Psalm 103:3). If you're carrying the weight of unforgiveness because someone has hurt you, stop hindering your own progress. Let go and let God — do your part to get over it and let God do His part to bring restoration to your life. This is one of my favorite sayings: When someone offends you, don't nurse it, don't rehearse it, but curse it, disperse it, and God will reverse it.

By faith, you can say, "Lord, Your love has been shed abroad in my heart by the Holy Ghost according to Romans 5:5. My thoughts are focused on things that are good, and I'm choosing to put my painful past behind me. I choose to forgive him (or her) in Jesus' name, and believe the best about them. I didn't have to let them cause me to lack

confidence and be insecure, but I did, so please forgive me too. Thank You, God."

#4 — Think on Things That are Lovely

One of the things I like about Jesus is that He never tells you to do something you cannot do. If He did, He would be unjust, and God is a just and faithful God! We can do what Philippians 4:8,9 says.

Finally, brethren, whatsoever things are true, whatsoever things are honest, whatsoever things are just, whatsoever things are pure, whatsoever things are lovely, whatsoever things are of good report; if there be any virtue, and if there be any praise, think on these things. Those things, which ye have both learned, and received, and heard, and seen in me, do: and the God of peace shall be with you.

Keep your mind filled with happy, peaceful thoughts, and let God take care of your problems!

#5 — Trust God

We can never trust God too much. We need to trust in Him in every situation. God has a good plan for our lives, and we partake in His plan through faith. Faith is trust in God. When we spend our lives trusting in ourselves and other people, we will be disappointed. People hurt other people, whether they mean to or not. But God will not hurt you. He can be trusted. Start speaking these "trust" scriptures over yourself:

Trust in the Lord, and do good; so shalt thou dwell in the land, and verily thou shalt be fed. Delight thyself also in the Lord; and he shall give thee the desires of thine heart. Commit thy way unto the Lord; trust also in him; and he shall bring it to pass. And he shall bring forth thy righteousness as the light, and thy judgment as the noonday.

— Psalm 37:3-6 KJV

Behold, God is my salvation; I will trust, and not be afraid: for the Lord Jehovah is my strength and my song; he also is become my salvation.

— Isaiah 12:2 KJV

As for God, his way is perfect; the word of the Lord is tried: he is a buckler to all them that trust in him. For who is God, save the Lord? and who is a rock, save our God?

— 2 Samuel 22:31,32 KJV

Trust in him at all times; ye people, pour out your heart before him: God is a refuge for us.

— Psalm 62:8 KJV

#6 — Surround Yourself With Encouragers

Watch out who you're spending time with. Your relationships are critical to the healing process, especially when you're dealing with insecurity, intimidation, fear, and rejection. Relax — you *are* capable of having healthy relationships with people even if you've been afraid of being hurt by people in the past.

Learning how to live free from intimidation and its effects takes the power of the Holy Spirit living inside of you. But you can be assured that victory is yours because...*greater is he that is in you, than he that is in the world* (1 John 4:4).

He that walketh with wise men shall be wise: but a companion of fools shall be destroyed.

— Proverbs 13:20 KJV

A friend loveth at all times, and a brother is born for adversity.

— Proverbs 17:17 KJV

Make no friendship with an angry man; and with a furious man thou shalt not go: lest thou learn his ways, and get a snare to thy soul.

— Proverbs 22:24,25 KJV

I am a companion of all them that fear thee, and of them that keep thy precepts.

— Psalm 119:63 KJV

#7 — Determine to Come Up Higher

In his letter to the Philippians while imprisoned in Rome, the apostle Paul remained determined to come up higher and overcome the weaknesses and inadequacies of his flesh, including the opportunity to give in to self-pity, fear, insecurity, and the rejection of men.

In the same way Paul rose above his circumstances, we need to strive to overcome. In Philippians 3:12-15, he says:

Not as though I had already attained, either were already perfect: but I follow after, if that I may apprehend that for which also I am apprehended of Christ Jesus. Brethren, I count not myself to have apprehended: but this one thing I do, forgetting those things which are behind, and reaching forth unto those things which are before, I press toward the mark for the prize of the high calling of God in Christ Jesus. Let us therefore, as many as be perfect, be thus minded: and if in any thing ye be otherwise minded, God shall reveal even this unto you.

Living in fear, insecurity, intimidation, and rejection does not help you to be your best. Even praying is difficult while you're still burdened with these bondages, much less responding to the full call of God on your life. He wants you to walk in victory. It will take hard work and a conscious decision to stick with it, but even if you slip up from time to time, keep pressing on and reaching up! He forgives us much quicker than we forgive ourselves. Stand up, shake it off, and hold your head high as you trust God to lead you to victory.

#8 — Peace Is Found in Believing

We must *believe* what God says about us. I strongly encourage you to meditate on these scriptures on acceptance until you believe them in your heart — and remember, they are descriptions of you:

> *For thou art an holy people unto the Lord thy God: the Lord thy God hath chosen thee to be a special people unto himself, above all people that are upon the face of the earth.*

— Deuteronomy 7:6 KJV

Know ye that the Lord he is God: it is he that hath made us, and not we ourselves; we are his people, and the sheep of his pasture.

— Psalm 100:3 KJV

The Lord hath appeared of old unto me, saying, Yea, I have loved thee with an everlasting love: therefore with lovingkindness have I drawn thee.

— Jeremiah 31:3 KJV

But now thus saith the Lord that created thee, O Jacob, and he that formed thee, O Israel, Fear not: for I have redeemed thee, I have called thee by thy name; thou art mine.

— Isaiah 43:1 KJV

#9 — Focus on Others

It is easy to keep our minds on ourselves when we're hurt, afraid, intimidated, and insecure, but healing won't come until we set aside ourselves and our problems and focus on others. When we're born again and have a relationship with Christ, we're given a supernatural desire to become more like Him, and Jesus was never self-centered. We need to learn to set aside what we want and want what God wants more. John 3:30 says, *He must increase, but I must decrease.* No matter how terrible our lives look to us, all we have to do is look around to discover someone going through something worse than anything we're facing.

True peace and joy come only as a result of giving of yourself. Find something to do that takes your mind off yourself. Look for someone who is alone, and visit with him or her — listen to them. So many people are searching for someone with whom they can share just a few moments of what might have been a very long day had you not come along.

> *Charity suffereth long, and is kind; charity envieth not; charity vaunteth not itself, is not puffed up, doth not behave itself unseemly, seeketh not her own, is not easily provoked, thinketh no evil; rejoiceth not in iniquity; but rejoiceth in the truth; beareth all things, believeth all things, hopeth all things, endureth all things.*
>
> — 1 Corinthians 13:4-7 KJV

#10 — The Joy of the Lord Is Your Strength

Then he said unto them, Go your way, eat the fat, and drink the sweet, and send portions unto them for whom nothing is prepared: for this day is holy

unto our Lord: neither be ye sorry; for the joy of the

Lord is your strength.

— Nehemiah 8:10 KJV

It may come as a shock to you right now, but life can be enjoyable — you can even learn to enjoy yours! Once you've determined to "get over" the events that have negatively affected your life and press on, you can allow the joy of the Lord to be your strength.

Even when you've suffered emotional wounds at the hands of insensitive people, you have a choice — you can start to enjoy your life or you can continue to be in misery. Choose joy!

Whether hurtful things happened to you ten years or ten minutes ago — why not just forget it and go on? God has called you to walk in faith — and faith operates now! You cannot enjoy life without it. Here are some great "joy" scriptures for you to adopt as your own:

Thou hast put gladness in my heart, more than in

the time that their corn and their wine increased.

— Psalm 4:7 KJV

Thy words were found, and I did eat them; and thy word was unto me the joy and rejoicing of mine heart: for I am called by thy name, O Lord God of hosts.

— Jeremiah 15:16 KJV

And ye now therefore have sorrow: but I will see you again, and your heart shall rejoice, and your joy no man taketh from you. And in that day ye shall ask me nothing. Verily, verily, I say unto you, Whatsoever ye shall ask the Father in my name, he will give it you. Hitherto have ye asked nothing in my name: ask, and ye shall receive, that your joy may be full.

— John 16:22-24 KJV

These things I have spoken unto you, that in me ye might have peace. In the world ye shall have tribulation: but be of good cheer; I have overcome the world.

— John 16:33 KJV

I encourage you to make the decision today to apply these ten steps (and God may give you even more) to overcoming bondage to fear, intimidation, anxiety, and rejection in your own life. Remember, miracles come in cans. You *can* learn to walk in the love of God, and you *can* live in His peace. Keep thanking God for giving you the victory over intimidation.

Intimidation *can* be conquered. Encourage yourself and refuse to give up. There may be times when you won't have anyone to encourage you, so encourage yourself and remember that God's Word says you are a victor — a winner! You *can* do all things through Christ who strengthens you, and that includes overcoming intimidation! You really *can* be all that God has called you to be!

When you have been hurt, rejected, or offended, it's natural to feel wounded and misunderstood, or you may feel resentful and angry toward that person. But regardless of how you feel, you will fall into the trap the devil has set for you if you don't make the decision to let it go.

Chapter Eight

SCRIPTURES TO
HELP YOU OVERCOME

SCRIPTURE TO HELP YOU OVERCOME

I can do all things through Christ which strengtheneth Me.

— Philippians 4:13 KJV

So we take comfort and are encouraged and confidently and boldly say, The Lord is my Helper; I will not be seized with alarm [I will not fear or dread or be terrified]. What can man do to me?

— Hebrews 13:6 AMP

Cast not away therefore your confidence, which hath great recompense of reward. For ye have need of patience, that, after ye have done the will of God,

ye might receive the promise.

— Hebrews 10:35,36 KJV

Being confident of this very thing, that he which hath

begun a good work in you will perform it until the

day of Jesus Christ.

— Philippians 1:6 KJV

The Lord God is my Strength, my personal bravery,

and my invincible army; He makes my feet like

hinds' feet and will make me to walk [not to stand

still in terror, but to walk] and make [spiritual]

progress upon my high places [of trouble, suffering,

or responsibility]!

— Habakkuk 3:19 AMP

Yet amid all these things we are more than con-

querors and gain a surpassing victory through Him

Who loved us.

— Romans 8:37 AMP

And this is the confidence that we have in him, that,

if we ask any thing according to his will, he heareth

us: and if we know that he hear us, whatsoever we ask, we know that we have the petitions that we desired of him.

— 1 John 5:14,15 KJV

Verily, verily, I say unto you, He that believeth on me, the works that I do shall he do also; and greater works than these shall he do; because I go unto my Father.

— John 14:12 KJV

Then he answered and spake unto me, saying, This is the word of the Lord unto Zerubbabel, saying, Not by might, nor by power, but by my spirit, saith the Lord of hosts.

— Zechariah 4:6 KJV

When thou passest through the waters, I will be with thee; and through the rivers, they shall not overflow thee: when thou walkest through the fire, thou shalt not be burned; neither shall the flame kindle upon thee.

— Isaiah 43:2 KJV

For the Lord shall be your confidence, firm and
strong, and shall keep your foot from being caught
[in a trap or some hidden danger].

— Proverbs 3:26 AMP

I rejoice therefore that I have confidence in you in all
things.

— 2 Corinthians 7:16 KJV

In whom we have boldness and access with confidence by the faith of him.

— Ephesians 3:12 KJV

And, beloved, if our consciences (our hearts) do not
accuse us [if they do not make us feel guilty and con-
demn us], we have confidence (complete assurance
and boldness) before God...

— 1 John 3:21 AMP

But they that wait upon the Lord shall renew their
strength; they shall mount up with wings as eagles;
they shall run, and not be weary; and they shall
walk, and not faint.

— Isaiah 40:31 KJV

In the fear of the Lord is strong confidence: and his children shall have a place of refuge.

— Proverbs 14:26 KJV

Preaching to them the kingdom of God and teaching them about the Lord Jesus Christ with boldness and quite openly, and without being molested or hindered.

— Acts 28:31 AMP

Do not, therefore, fling away your fearless confidence, for it carries a great and glorious compensation of reward.

— Hebrews 10:35 AMP

And we know that all things work together for good to them that love God, to them who are the called according to his purpose.

— Romans 8:28 KJV

I will lift up mine eyes unto the hills, from whence cometh my help. My help cometh from the Lord, which made heaven and earth.

— Psalm 121:1,2 KJV

What shall we then say to these things? If God be for
us, who can be against us?

— Romans 8:31 KJV

Be strong, courageous, and firm; fear not nor be in
terror before them, for it is the Lord your God Who
goes with you; He will not fail you or forsake you.

— Deuteronomy 31:6 AMP

For the Lord will not forsake his people for his great
name's sake: because it hath pleased the Lord to
make you his people.

— 1 Samuel 12:22 KJV

The Lord will perfect that which concerneth me: thy
mercy, O Lord, endureth for ever: forsake not the
works of thine own hands.

— Psalm 138:8 KJV

Fear thou not; for I am with thee: be not dismayed;
for I am thy God: I will strengthen thee; yea, I will
help thee; yea, I will uphold thee with the right hand
of my righteousness.

— Isaiah 41:10 KJV

Let us hold fast the profession of our faith without wavering; (for he is faithful that promised;)

— Hebrews 10:23 KJV

Thou wilt keep him in perfect peace, whose mind is stayed on thee: because he trusteth in thee.

— Isaiah 26:3 KJV

Thou hast granted me life and favour, and thy visitation hath preserved my spirit.

— Job 10:12 KJV

To the praise of the glory of his grace, wherein he hath made us accepted in the beloved.

— Ephesians 1:6 KJV

Let us therefore come boldly unto the throne of grace, that we may obtain mercy, and find grace to help in time of need.

— Hebrews 4:16 KJV

Be of good courage, and he shall strengthen your heart, all ye that hope in the Lord.

— Psalm 31:24 KJV

The Lord is my rock, and my fortress, and my deliverer; my God, my strength, in whom I will trust; my buckler, and the horn of my salvation, and my high tower.

— Psalm 18:2 KJV

The Lord is my light and my salvation; whom shall I fear? the Lord is the strength of my life; of whom shall I be afraid?

— Psalm 27:1 KJV

The name of the Lord is a strong tower: the righteous runneth into it, and is safe.

— Proverbs 18:10 KJV

The eternal God is thy refuge, and underneath are the everlasting arms: and he shall thrust out the enemy from before thee; and shall say, Destroy them.

— Deuteronomy 33:27 KJV

My son, attend to my words; incline thine ear unto my sayings. Let them not depart from thine eyes; keep them in the midst of thine heart. For they are

life unto those that find them, and health to all their
flesh.

— Proverbs 4:20-22 KJV

He restoreth my soul: he leadeth me in the paths of
righteousness for his name's sake.

— Psalm 23:3 KJV

And ye shall know the truth, and the truth shall
make you free.

— John 8:32 KJV

Thy word is a lamp unto my feet, and a light unto
my path.

— Psalm 119:105 KJV

Nay, in all these things we are more than con-
querors through him that loved us.

— Romans 8:37 KJV

Your Daily Confession

This should be what you say about yourself every day:
"I am strong in the Lord and in the power of His might.
The Lord is my confidence, and my confidence comes from Him.

I am a child of the most high God. Therefore I will hold my head up high and be all that He has called me to be. The righteous are as bold as a lion, and I believe that I am as bold as a lion. I am not afraid of people or what they think about me.

"I am accepted in the beloved. I am highly favored of God. I am anointed to share the Good News, and I can do all things through Christ who strengthens me. The Greater One lives on the inside of me. The mighty Holy Spirit is living in me. I'm an overcomer. I am the head and not the tail. I am above and not beneath.

"I am more than a conqueror. I always triumph in Christ. I am confident, courageous, and strong in the Lord."

Always remember, friend, the Holy Spirit is living in you, and He is your confidence.

PRAYER FOR SALVATION

PRAYER FOR SALVATION

God cares for you and wants to help you overcome in every area of your life. That's why He sent Jesus to die for you.

If you have never received Jesus Christ as your personal Savior, you can make your heart right with God at this very moment. In doing so, you will make heaven your eternal home.

Pray this prayer from your heart:

O God, I ask You to forgive me of my sins. I believe You sent Jesus to die on the cross for me. I receive Jesus Christ as my personal Savior. I confess Him as Lord of my life, and I give my life to Him. Thank You, Lord, for saving me and for making me new. In Jesus' name, amen.

If you prayed this prayer for the first time, I welcome you to the family of God! Please write to me at the address on the following page and let me know about your decision for Jesus. I'd like to send you some free literature to help you in your walk with the Lord.

10 Benefits of Walking in the
Favor of God

FAVOR produces supernatural increase and promotion. . . Gen. 39:21

FAVOR produces restoration of everything that the enemy has stolen from you. . . EX. 3:21

FAVOR produces honor in the midst of your adversaries. . . Ex. 11:3

FAVOR produces increased assets, especially in the area of real estate. . . Dt. 33:23

FAVOR produces great victories in the midst of great impossibilities. . . Jos. 11:20

FAVOR produces recognition, even when you seem the least likely to receive it. . . 1 Sam. 16:22

FAVOR produces prominence and preferential treatment. . . Est. 2:17

FAVOR produces petitions granted even by ungodly civil authorities. . . Est. 5:8

FAVOR causes policies, rules, regulations, and laws to be changed and reversed to your advantage. . . Est. 8:5

FAVOR produces battles won which you won't even fight because God will fight them for you. . . Ps. 44:3

FOR FURTHER INFORMATION

FOR FURTHER INFORMATION

To receive:

- additional copies of this book
- a complete catalog of Rev. Kate McVeigh's books and tapes
- a free subscription to her bimonthly newsletter
- information regarding Kate's ministry schedule

please write or call:

Kate McVeigh Ministries

P.O. Box 1688

Warren, MI 48090

1-800-40-FAITH (1-800-403-2484)

Visit our website at:

www.KateMcVeigh.org

*Please include your prayer requests
and comments when you write.*